ROLAND PARKER

Learn Python programming, Fast and SIMPLIFIED

Python Programming For Beginners

Contents

Chapter 1: Introduction to Python

What is Python?

Python is a high-level, interpreted programming language that has gained immense popularity in recent years. Created by Guido van Rossum and first released in 1991, Python has evolved to become one of the most versatile and widely-used programming languages in the world.

At its core, Python is designed to be easy to read and write, with a syntax that emphasizes code readability and reduces the cost of program maintenance. It supports multiple programming paradigms, including:

1. **Procedural programming**: Writing code as a sequence of steps to be executed.
2. **Object-oriented programming (OOP)**: Organizing code into objects that contain data and code.
3. **Functional programming**: Treating computation as the evaluation of mathematical functions.

Python is often described as a "batteries included" language due to its comprehensive standard library, which provides modules and packages for a wide range of tasks. This extensive library, combined with Python's simplicity and versatility, makes it an excellent choice for beginners and experienced programmers alike.

Key Features of Python

1. **Interpreted Language**: Python code is executed line by line, rather than compiled all at once. This allows for rapid development and easier debugging.
2. **Dynamic Typing**: Variables in Python are not bound to a specific data type, allowing for more flexible code writing.
3. **Automatic Memory Management**: Python uses a garbage collector to automatically manage memory allocation and deallocation, reducing the risk of memory leaks.
4. **Cross-platform Compatibility**: Python can run on various operating systems, including Windows, macOS, and Linux, with minimal to no changes in the code.
5. **Extensive Libraries**: Python's standard library and third-party packages cover a vast range of functionalities, from web development to scientific computing.
6. **Community Support**: Python has a large, active community that contributes to its development, creates third-party packages, and provides support through forums and documentation.

Applications of Python

Python's versatility makes it suitable for a wide range of applications:

1. **Web Development**: Frameworks like Django and Flask make Python a popular choice for building web applications.
2. **Data Science and Machine Learning**: Libraries such as NumPy, Pandas, and Scikit-learn have made Python the go-to language for data analysis and machine learning.
3. **Artificial Intelligence**: Python's simplicity and powerful libraries make it ideal for AI development.
4. **Scientific Computing**: Python is widely used in scientific and numerical computing, with libraries like SciPy and Matplotlib.

5. **Automation and Scripting**: Python's ease of use makes it excellent for writing scripts to automate tasks.
6. **Game Development**: Libraries like Pygame allow developers to create 2D games with Python.
7. **Desktop Applications**: Python can be used to create GUI applications using libraries like Tkinter or PyQt.

Python's Philosophy and Advantages

Python's design philosophy is encapsulated in "The Zen of Python," a collection of 19 guiding principles for writing computer programs that influence the design of the Python programming language. These principles emphasize clarity, simplicity, and readability.

The Zen of Python

You can access the full Zen of Python by running import this in a Python interpreter. Here are some key principles:

1. **Beautiful is better than ugly.**
2. **Explicit is better than implicit.**
3. **Simple is better than complex.**
4. **Complex is better than complicated.**
5. **Readability counts.**
6. **Special cases aren't special enough to break the rules.**
7. **Errors should never pass silently.**
8. **In the face of ambiguity, refuse the temptation to guess.**
9. **There should be one— and preferably only one —obvious way to do it.**

These principles guide Python's development and encourage programmers to write clean, readable, and maintainable code.

Advantages of Python

Python offers numerous advantages that contribute to its popularity:

1. **Readability and Simplicity**: Python's syntax is clear and intuitive, making it easy to learn and read. It uses indentation to define code blocks, which enforces a consistent and readable code structure.
2. **Productivity**: Python's simplicity and extensive libraries allow developers to write code quickly and efficiently. This high productivity makes it an excellent choice for rapid prototyping and development.
3. **Versatility**: Python's "batteries included" philosophy and vast ecosystem of third-party packages make it suitable for a wide range of applications, from web development to scientific computing.
4. **Large and Active Community**: Python has a vast, supportive community that contributes to its development, creates third-party packages, and provides help through forums and documentation.
5. **Cross-platform Compatibility**: Python code can run on various operating systems with minimal to no changes, making it highly portable.
6. **Strong Integration Features**: Python can easily integrate with other languages like C, C++, and Java, allowing developers to use Python as a glue language to connect diverse components.
7. **Open Source**: Python is open-source, which means it's free to use and distribute, even for commercial purposes.
8. **Extensive Libraries**: Python's standard library and third-party packages provide tools for a wide range of tasks, reducing the need to write code from scratch.
9. **Scalability**: Despite being an interpreted language, Python can be used to build large, complex applications. Companies like Google, Netflix, and Dropbox use Python extensively in their technology stacks.
10. **Career Opportunities**: The growing popularity of Python has led to increased demand for Python developers across various industries, offering excellent career prospects.

Setting up Your Python Environment

To start programming in Python, you need to set up your development environment. This process involves installing Python on your computer and optionally setting up additional tools to enhance your coding experience.

Step 1: Installing Python

1. **Windows**:

- Visit the official Python website (https://www.python.org/downloads/).
- Download the latest version of Python for Windows.
- Run the installer, ensuring you check the box that says "Add Python to PATH" during installation.

1. **macOS**:

- macOS usually comes with Python pre-installed. However, it's often an older version.
- To install the latest version, you can use Homebrew (a package manager for macOS):
- Install Homebrew if you haven't already: /bin/bash -c "$(curl -fsSL https://raw.githubusercontent.com/Homebrew/install/HEAD/install.sh)"
- Install Python: brew install python

1. **Linux**:

- Most Linux distributions come with Python pre-installed.
- To install the latest version, use your distribution's package manager. For example, on Ubuntu or Debian:

```
Copy
sudo apt update
sudo apt install python3
```

Step 2: Verifying the Installation

After installation, open a terminal (Command Prompt on Windows) and type:

```
Copy
python --version
```

This should display the installed Python version. If you see an error, make sure Python is correctly added to your system's PATH.

Step 3: Choosing an Integrated Development Environment (IDE) or Text Editor

While you can write Python code in any text editor, using an IDE or a code-specific text editor can significantly enhance your coding experience. Here are some popular options:

1. **PyCharm**: A full-featured IDE specifically designed for Python development.
2. **Visual Studio Code**: A lightweight, extensible code editor with excellent Python support through extensions.
3. **Jupyter Notebook**: An open-source web application that allows you to create and share documents containing live code, equations, visualizations, and narrative text.
4. **IDLE**: A basic IDE that comes bundled with Python, suitable for beginners.

Step 4: Setting Up a Virtual Environment

Virtual environments are isolated Python environments that allow you to install packages and manage dependencies for specific projects without affecting your system-wide Python installation. Here's how to set up a virtual environment:

1. Open a terminal or command prompt.
2. Navigate to your project directory.
3. Create a virtual environment:

```
Copy
python -m venv myenv
```

1. Activate the virtual environment:

- On Windows: myenv\Scripts\activate
- On macOS and Linux: source myenv/bin/activate

When activated, your terminal prompt will change to show the name of your virtual environment.

Step 5: Installing Packages

Python's package manager, pip, allows you to easily install third-party packages. With your virtual environment activated:

1. Upgrade pip:

```
Copy
pip install --upgrade pip
```

1. Install a package (e.g., NumPy):

```
Copy
pip install numpy
```

Step 6: Writing Your First Python Program

Now that your environment is set up, you can write your first Python program:

1. Open your chosen IDE or text editor.
2. Create a new file and save it with a .py extension (e.g., hello_world.py).
3. Type the following code:

```python
Copy
print("Hello, World!")
```

1. Save the file and run it:

- In the terminal: python hello_world.py
- Or use your IDE's run function.

Congratulations! You've just run your first Python program.

Conclusion

Python's simplicity, versatility, and powerful features make it an excellent choice for beginners and experienced programmers alike. Its clear syntax and "batteries included" philosophy allow developers to quickly write efficient, readable code for a wide range of applications.

As you embark on your Python journey, remember that the key to mastering any programming language is practice. Experiment with different concepts, work on small projects, and don't hesitate to seek help from the vast Python community when you encounter challenges.

In the following chapters, we'll go deeper into Python's syntax, data structures, control flow, and more advanced features, providing you with the knowledge and skills to become a proficient Python programmer.

Chapter 2: Python Basics: Syntax and Variables

Writing Your First Python Program

Now that we've set up our Python environment, let's dive into writing our first Python program. We'll start with the classic "Hello, World!" example and then gradually introduce more complex concepts.

Hello, World!

1. Open your preferred text editor or Integrated Development Environment (IDE).
2. Create a new file and name it hello_world.py.
3. Type the following code:

```python
Copy
print("Hello, World!")
```

1. Save the file.

2. Open a terminal or command prompt, navigate to the directory containing your file, and run:

```
Copy
python hello_world.py
```

You should see "Hello, World!" printed to the console. Congratulations! You've just written and executed your first Python program.

Breaking Down the Hello World Program

Let's analyze this simple program:

1. print() is a built-in Python function that outputs text to the console.
2. The text to be printed is enclosed in parentheses () and quotation marks "".
3. In Python, strings (text) can be enclosed in either single " or double "" quotes.

A Slightly More Complex Program

Now, let's write a program that asks for the user's name and greets them:

```python
Copy
# Ask for the user's name
name = input("What's your name? ")

# Greet the user
print(f"Hello, {name}!
  Welcome to Python programming.")
```

This program introduces several new concepts:

1. input() is a function that prompts the user for input.
2. We store the user's input in a variable called name.
3. We use an f-string (formatted string literal) to include the name variable in our greeting.
4. The # symbol is used for comments in Python. Comments are ignored by the Python interpreter and are used to explain the code.

Understanding Python Syntax

Python's syntax is designed to be clear and readable. Let's explore some key aspects of Python's syntax.

Indentation

Unlike many other programming languages that use braces {} to define code blocks, Python uses indentation. This enforces clean, readable code. For example:

```python
Copy
if True:
print("This is indented")
print("This is also indented")
print("This is not indented")
```

In this example, the first two print statements are part of the if block because they are indented. The third print statement is not indented, so it's not part of the if block.

Comments

Python supports single-line and multi-line comments:

```python
Copy
# This is a single-line comment

"""
This is a multi-line comment
It can span several lines
"""
```

Statements and Lines

In Python, a statement is typically written on a single line:

```python
Copy
x = 5
y = 10
z = x + y
```

However, you can use a backslash \ for line continuation if needed:

```python
Copy
long_calculation = \
  1 + 2 + 3 + 4 + \
    5 + 6 + 7 + 8
```

For lists, tuples, and dictionaries, you don't need the backslash:

```python
Copy
fruits = [
    "apple",
    "banana",
    "cherry"
```

]

Semicolons

Unlike some other languages, Python doesn't require semicolons at the end of statements. However, you can use them to put multiple statements on one line:

```python
Copy
x = 5; y = 10; print(x + y)
```

This practice is generally discouraged as it can make code less readable.

Variables and Data Types

Variables are used to store data in a computer program. In Python, you don't need to declare a variable's type explicitly; Python determines it automatically based on the value assigned.

Variable Naming Rules

1. Variable names can contain letters, numbers, and underscores.
2. They must start with a letter or underscore.
3. Names are case-sensitive (myVar and myvar are different variables).
4. You cannot use Python keywords as variable names.

Good practice:

- Use descriptive names (e.g., user_age instead of ua).
- Use lowercase letters and underscores for variable names (snake_case).
- Be consistent in your naming conventions.

Assigning Values to Variables

In Python, you use the = operator to assign values to variables:

```python
Copy
x = 5
name = "Alice"
is_student = True
```

You can also assign values to multiple variables in one line:

```python
Copy
a, b, c = 1, 2, 3
```

Basic Data Types

Python has several built-in data types. Let's explore the most common ones:

1. **Integers (int)**: Whole numbers, positive or negative.

```python
Copy
age = 25
year = 2023
```

1. **Floating-point numbers (float)**: Numbers with decimal points.

```python
Copy
height = 1.75
pi = 3.14159
```

1. **Strings (str)**: Sequences of characters, enclosed in quotes.

```python
Copy
name = "Bob"
message = 'Hello, World!'
```

1. **Booleans (bool)**: Represent True or False values.

```python
Copy
is_raining = False
has_passed = True
```

1. **None**: Represents the absence of a value.

```python
Copy
result = None
```

Type Conversion

You can convert between different data types using built-in functions:

```python
Copy
# String to Integer
age_str = "25"
age_int = int(age_str)

# Integer to String
number = 42
number_str = str(number)

# String to Float
price_str = "19.99"
price_float = float(price_str)
```

Checking Variable Types

You can use the type() function to check the type of a variable:

```python
Copy
x = 5
y = "Hello"
z = 3.14

print(type(x))  # <class 'int'>
print(type(y))  # <class 'str'>
print(type(z))  # <class 'float'>
```

Complex Data Types

Python also has several complex data types that can hold multiple values:

1. **Lists**: Ordered, mutable sequences of values.

```python
Copy
fruits = ["apple",
"banana", "cherry"]
```

1. **Tuples**: Ordered, immutable sequences of values.

```python
Copy
coordinates = (10, 20)
```

1. **Dictionaries**: Unordered collections of key-value pairs.

```python
Copy
person = {"name": "Alice",
  "age": 30, "city":
"New York"}
```

1. **Sets**: Unordered collections of unique elements.

```python
Copy
unique_numbers =
{1, 2, 3, 4, 5}
```

We'll explore these complex data types in more detail in later chapters.

Variables and Memory

When you create a variable in Python, you're essentially creating a reference to an object in memory. Let's look at an example:

```python
Copy
x = 5
y = x
```

In this case, both x and y refer to the same integer object with the value 5. If we change the value of x, it doesn't affect y:

```python
Copy
x = 10
print(x)   # 10
print(y)   # 5
```

This behavior is different for mutable objects like lists:

```python
Copy
a = [1, 2, 3]
b = a
b.append(4)
print(a)   # [1, 2, 3, 4]
print(b)   # [1, 2, 3, 4]
```

In this case, both a and b refer to the same list object, so changes to b are reflected in a.

Constants

Python doesn't have built-in constant types, but by convention, we use all uppercase names for values that shouldn't be changed:

```python
Copy
PI = 3.14159
MAX_USERS = 100
```

While these can still be reassigned, the all-caps naming signals to other programmers that these values shouldn't be modified.

Practical Examples

Let's put our knowledge of Python basics into practice with a few examples:

Example 1: Temperature Converter

This program converts temperatures from Fahrenheit to Celsius:

```python
Copy
# Get temperature in Fahrenheit
from user
fahrenheit = float(input
("Enter temperature in
 Fahrenheit: "))

# Convert to Celsius
celsius = (fahrenheit - 32) * 5/9
```

```
# Print the result
print(f"{fahrenheit}
°F is equal to {celsius:.2f}°C")
```

This program demonstrates:

- Using input() to get user input
- Converting strings to floats
- Performing calculations
- Using f-strings for formatted output
- Rounding to two decimal places with .2f

Example 2: Simple Calculator

Let's create a basic calculator that can add, subtract, multiply, or divide two numbers:

```python
Copy
# Get two numbers and operation from user
num1 = float(input
("Enter first number: "))
num2 = float(input
("Enter second number: "))
operation = input(
"Enter operation (+, -, *, /): ")

# Perform calculation based on operation
if operation == "+":
    result = num1 + num2
elif operation == "-":
    result = num1 - num2
elif operation == "*":
    result = num1 * num2
elif operation == "/":
if num2 != 0:
```

```
result = num1 / num2
    else:
result = "Error:
 Division by zero"
else:
result = "Error:
Invalid operation"

# Print the result
print(f"Result: {result}")
```

This program introduces:

- Conditional statements (if, elif, else)
- Handling potential errors (division by zero)
- More complex user interaction

Conclusion

In this chapter, we've covered the fundamental building blocks of Python programming: basic syntax, variables, and data types. We've learned how to write simple programs, understand Python's indentation-based structure, work with different types of data, and apply these concepts in practical examples.

As you continue your Python journey, you'll build upon these basics to create more complex and powerful programs. Remember, the key to mastering programming is practice. Experiment with the concepts we've covered, try modifying the example programs, and create your own small projects to reinforce your learning.

In the next chapter, we'll explore control flow in Python, including if statements and loops, which will allow you to create more dynamic and responsive programs.

Chapter 3: Control Flow: Making Decisions

Control flow is a fundamental concept in programming that allows you to control the execution of your code based on certain conditions. In this chapter, we'll explore the key control flow structures in Python: if statements, loops, and control flow modifiers like break and continue.

If Statements

If statements allow you to execute different blocks of code based on whether a condition is true or false. They are the foundation of decision-making in programming.

Basic If Statement

The simplest form of an if statement looks like this:

```python
Copy
if condition:
    # code to execute
if condition is True
```

For example:

```
python
Copy
age = 18
if age >= 18:
print("You are an adult.")
```

If-Else Statement

You can use an else clause to specify what should happen if the condition is False:

```
python
Copy
age = 16
if age >= 18:
print("You are an adult.")
else:
print("You are a minor.")
```

If-Elif-Else Statement

For multiple conditions, you can use elif (short for "else if"):

```
python
Copy
score = 85

if score >= 90:
    print("A")
elif score >= 80:
    print("B")
elif score >= 70:
```

```python
    print("C")
elif score >= 60:
    print("D")
else:
    print("F")
```

Nested If Statements

You can also nest if statements inside other if statements:

```python
python
Copy
x = 10
y = 5

if x > 0:
    if y > 0:
print("Both x and y are positive")
    else:
print("x is positive, but y is not")
else:
print("x is not positive")
```

Ternary Operator

Python offers a concise way to write simple if-else statements in a single line, known as the ternary operator:

```python
python
Copy
age = 20
status = "adult" if age
 >= 18 else "minor"
```

```
print(status)  # Output: adult
```

Truthy and Falsy Values

In Python, values can be evaluated as either "truthy" or "falsy" in boolean contexts. Here are some falsy values:

- False
- None
- Zero of any numeric type (0, 0.0)
- Empty sequences (", [], ())
- Empty mappings ({})

All other values are considered truthy. This allows for concise conditional checks:

```python
Copy
name = " "
if name:
print("Name is not empty")
else:
print("Name is empty")
```

Loops

Loops allow you to repeat a block of code multiple times. Python provides two main types of loops: for loops and while loops.

For Loops

For loops are used to iterate over a sequence (like a list, tuple, string, or range) or other iterable objects.

Basic For Loop

```python
Copy
fruits = ["apple",
"banana", "cherry"]
for fruit in fruits:
    print(fruit)
```

Using range()

The range() function is commonly used with for loops to repeat an action a specific number of times:

```python
Copy
for i in range(5):
print(i)  #
Prints 0, 1, 2, 3, 4
```

You can also specify start, stop, and step values:

```python
Copy
for i in range(2, 10, 2):
print(i)  # Prints
2, 4, 6, 8
```

Looping Through Dictionaries

You can loop through dictionaries using the items() method:

```python
Copy
person = {"name": "Alice",
"age": 30, "city": "New York"}
for key, value in person.items():
print(f"{key}: {value}")
```

Enumerate

The enumerate() function allows you to loop over a sequence while keeping track of the index:

```python
Copy
fruits = ["apple", "banana", "cherry"]
for index, fruit
  in enumerate(fruits):
print(f"{index}: {fruit}")
```

While Loops

While loops repeat a block of code as long as a condition is True.

Basic While Loop

```python
Copy
```

```
count = 0
while count < 5:
    print(count)
    count += 1
```

Infinite Loops

Be careful not to create unintended infinite loops. Always ensure there's a way for the loop condition to become False:

```
python
Copy
# This is an infinite loop
(don't run this!)
# while True:
#print("This will go on forever!")

# This is better:
count = 0
while True:
print(count)
count += 1
if count >= 5:
        break
```

Break and Continue Statements

Break and continue statements provide additional control within loops.

Break Statement

The break statement immediately terminates the loop it's in:

```python
Copy
for i in range(10):
    if i == 5:
        break
    print(i)  # Prints
0, 1, 2, 3, 4
```

It's often used with while loops to exit based on a condition:

```python
Copy
while True:
    response = input("Enter
 'quit' to exit: ")
if response.lower() == 'quit':
        break
print("You entered:", response)
```

Continue Statement

The continue statement skips the rest of the current iteration and moves to the next one:

```python
Copy
for i in range(5):
    if i == 2:
        continue
print(i)  # Prints 0, 1, 3, 4
```

It's useful for skipping certain elements in a loop:

```python
Copy
numbers = [1, 2, 3, 4,
  5, 6, 7, 8, 9, 10]
for num in numbers:
if num % 2 == 0:
        continue
print(num)  # Prints only odd numbers
```

Combining Control Flow Structures

You can combine these control flow structures to create more complex logic.
Let's look at some examples:

Example 1: Finding Prime Numbers

This program finds prime numbers up to a given limit:

```python
Copy
limit = 20
print(f"Prime numbers up to
  {limit}:")

for num in range(2, limit + 1):
for i in range(2, int
(num ** 0.5) + 1):
if num % i == 0:
            break
    else:
print(num, end=" ")
```

This example demonstrates:

- Nested loops
- The use of break

- The else clause of a for loop (which runs if the loop completes without a break)

Example 2: Simple Menu System

Here's a program that implements a simple menu system:

```python
Copy
while True:
print("\nMenu:")
print("1. Say hello")
print("2. Count to 10")
print("3. Exit")

choice = input
("Enter your choice (1-3): ")

    if choice == '1':
print("Hello, World!")
elif choice == '2':
for i in range(1, 11):
print(i, end=" ")
        print()
elif choice == '3':
print("Goodbye!")
        break
    else:
print("Invalid choice.
 Please try again.")
```

This example shows:

- A while loop for the main program loop
- If-elif-else for menu choices
- A for loop within a menu option
- Using break to exit the program

Advanced Control Flow Concepts

As you become more comfortable with basic control flow, you can explore some more advanced concepts:

List Comprehensions

List comprehensions provide a concise way to create lists based on existing lists:

```python
Copy
numbers = [1, 2, 3, 4, 5]
squares = [x**2 for x
 in numbers if x % 2 == 0]
print(squares)  # Output: [4, 16]
```

Try-Except Blocks

Try-except blocks allow you to handle potential errors gracefully:

```python
Copy
try:
    x = int(input("Enter
a number: "))
    result = 10 / x
print("Result:", result)
except ValueError:
    print("Please enter
a valid number.")
except ZeroDivisionError:
    print("Cannot divide by
zero.")
except Exception as e:
```

```
    print("An error
occurred:", str(e))
```

With Statements

With statements are used for resource management, ensuring that certain operations are performed after the code block is executed:

```python
Copy
with open("example.txt", "w") as file:
file.write("Hello, World!")
# File is automatically
 closed after the block
```

Best Practices for Control Flow

When working with control flow structures, keep these best practices in mind:

1. **Keep it simple**: Avoid overly complex nested structures. If your code becomes hard to follow, consider breaking it into functions.
2. **Use meaningful names**: Choose descriptive names for variables and functions to make your code self-explanatory.
3. **Comment your code**: Add comments to explain complex logic or the purpose of certain blocks.
4. **Be consistent**: Stick to a consistent style for indentation and formatting.
5. **Avoid deep nesting**: Try to limit the depth of nested structures to maintain readability.
6. **Use elif instead of multiple if statements**: When checking multiple conditions, use elif for clarity and efficiency.
7. **Consider the else clause**: Remember that else can be used with both if

statements and loops.

8. **Be careful with infinite loops**: Ensure there's always a way to exit a while loop.

9. **Use break and continue judiciously**: While useful, overuse can make code harder to follow.

10. **Consider using functions**: If a piece of logic is repeated or complex, consider moving it to a separate function.

Conclusion

Control flow is a crucial aspect of programming that allows you to create dynamic and responsive programs. By mastering if statements, loops, and control flow modifiers like break and continue, you'll be able to write more sophisticated Python programs that can make decisions and handle various scenarios.

Remember that the key to becoming proficient with control flow is practice. Try to solve problems using different combinations of these structures, and don't be afraid to experiment. As you gain experience, you'll develop an intuition for which control flow structures are best suited for different situations.

In the next chapter, we'll explore functions, which will allow you to organize your code into reusable blocks and further enhance your ability to create complex programs.

Chapter 4: Functions: Reusable Code Blocks

F unctions are a fundamental building block in Python programming. They allow you to organize your code into reusable blocks, making your programs more modular, easier to understand, and simpler to maintain. In this chapter, we'll explore how to define and use functions, work with parameters and return values, and understand the scope and lifetime of variables within functions.

Defining and Calling Functions

Basic Function Definition

In Python, you define a function using the def keyword, followed by the function name and a pair of parentheses. Here's the basic syntax:

```python
Copy
def function_name():
    # Function body
# Code to be executed
```

Let's create a simple function that prints a greeting:

```python
Copy
def greet():
print("Hello, World!")

# Calling the function
greet()  # Output: Hello, World!
```

Function Names

Function names follow the same rules as variable names:

- They can contain letters, numbers, and underscores
- They must start with a letter or underscore
- They are case-sensitive
- They cannot be Python keywords

It's good practice to use descriptive names for your functions, using lowercase letters and underscores to separate words (snake_case).

Calling Functions

To execute a function, you simply write its name followed by parentheses:

```python
Copy
greet()
```

You can call a function as many times as you need in your program.

Parameters and Return Values

Functions become much more powerful when they can accept input (parameters) and provide output (return values).

Parameters

Parameters allow you to pass data into a function. You define parameters in the parentheses when you create the function:

```python
Copy
def greet(name):
print(f"Hello, {name}!")

greet("Alice")
 # Output: Hello, Alice!
greet("Bob")
# Output: Hello, Bob!
```

You can have multiple parameters:

```python
Copy
def describe_pet(animal_type,
 pet_name):
print(f"I have a {animal_type}
 named {pet_name}.")

describe_pet("dog", "Rex")
describe_pet("cat",
 "Whiskers")
```

Default Parameter Values

You can provide default values for parameters, which are used if the caller doesn't provide a value:

```python
Copy
def greet(name="Guest"):
print(f"Hello, {name}!")

greet()
 # Output: Hello, Guest!
greet("Alice")
 # Output: Hello, Alice!
```

Keyword Arguments

When calling a function, you can specify which parameter each argument corresponds to:

```python
Copy
def describe_pet(animal_type,
 pet_name):
print(f"I have a
{animal_type} named {pet_name}
.")

describe_pet(animal_type=
"hamster", pet_name="Fluffy")
describe_pet(pet_name=
"Whiskers", animal_type="cat")
```

This is especially useful for functions with many parameters or when you want to provide arguments out of order.

Arbitrary Number of Arguments

You can create functions that accept any number of arguments using *args for positional arguments and **kwargs for keyword arguments:

```python
Copy
def print_args(*args):
for arg in args:
print(arg)

print_args(1, 2, 3, "hello")

def print_kwargs(**kwargs):
for key, value in kwargs.items():
print(f"{key}: {value}")

print_kwargs(name="Alice",
age=30, city="New York")
```

Return Values

Functions can send data back to the caller using the return statement:

```python
Copy
def add(a, b):
    return a + b

result = add(3, 5)
print(result)  # Output: 8
```

A function can return multiple values as a tuple:

```python
Copy
def get_min_max(numbers):
    return min(numbers), max(numbers)

min_val, max_val = get_min
_max([1, 5, 3, 9, 2])
print(f"Min: {min_val}, Max:
{max_val}")  # Output:
 Min: 1, Max: 9
```

If a function doesn't explicitly return a value, it implicitly returns None:

```python
Copy
def greet(name):
print(f"Hello, {name}!")

result = greet("Alice")
print(result)  # Output: None
```

Scope and Lifetime of Variables

Understanding variable scope is crucial when working with functions. The scope of a variable determines where in your code the variable can be accessed.

Local Scope

Variables defined inside a function have a local scope. They can only be accessed within that function:

```python
Copy
```

```
def my_function():
    x = 10
    print(x)

my_function()  # Output: 10
print(x)  # This will raise a NameError
```

Global Scope

Variables defined outside of any function have a global scope and can be accessed from anywhere in the module:

```
python
Copy
y = 20

def print_global():
    print(y)

print_global()  # Output: 20
```

The global Keyword

If you want to modify a global variable from within a function, you need to use the global keyword:

```
python
Copy
counter = 0

def increment():
    global counter
    counter += 1
```

```
increment()
print(counter)   # Output: 1
```

However, it's generally better to avoid modifying global variables from within functions, as it can lead to code that's harder to understand and debug.

Nonlocal Variables

In nested functions, you can use the nonlocal keyword to work with variables in the nearest enclosing scope:

```python
Copy
def outer():
    x = "outer"
def inner():
nonlocal x
x = "inner"
    inner()
print(x)   # Output: inner

outer()
```

Variable Lifetime

The lifetime of a variable is the duration for which the variable exists in memory:

- Global variables live for the entire duration of the program.
- Local variables are created when the function is called and destroyed when the function exits.

Advanced Function Concepts

As you become more comfortable with basic function usage, you can explore some more advanced concepts:

Lambda Functions

Lambda functions are small, anonymous functions that can have any number of arguments but can only have one expression:

```python
Copy
square = lambda x: x ** 2
print(square(5))  # Output: 25

# Using lambda with built-
in functions
numbers = [1, 5, 3, 9, 2]
sorted_numbers = sorted
(numbers, key=lambda x:

abs(x - 5))
print(sorted_numbers)
 # Output: [5, 3, 2, 1, 9]
```

Decorators

Decorators allow you to modify or enhance functions without changing their code:

```python
Copy
def uppercase_decorator(func):
    def wrapper():
result = func()
```

```
    return result.upper()
    return wrapper

@uppercase_decorator
def greet():
return "hello, world!"

print(greet())  # Output:
HELLO, WORLD!
```

Generators

Generators are functions that use the yield keyword to return a generator iterator:

```python
Copy
def countdown(n):
    while n > 0:
        yield n
        n -= 1

for number in countdown(5):
print(number)
 # Output: 5 4 3 2 1
```

Best Practices for Functions

When working with functions, keep these best practices in mind:

1. **Do one thing well**: Each function should have a single, well-defined purpose.
2. **Keep functions small**: Aim for functions that are short and focused. If a function gets too long, consider breaking it into smaller functions.

3. **Use descriptive names**: Choose function names that clearly describe what the function does.

4. **Document your functions**: Use docstrings to explain what your function does, its parameters, and what it returns:

```python
python
Copy
def calculate_area(length, width):
    """

Calculate the area of a rectangle.

    Args:
length (float): The length of the rectangle.
width (float): The width of the rectangle.

    Returns:
float: The area of the rectangle.
    """
    return length * width
```

1. **Handle errors gracefully**: Use try-except blocks to catch and handle potential errors.

2. **Avoid global variables**: Try to minimize the use of global variables in functions.

3. **Use default arguments carefully**: Be aware that default arguments are evaluated only once, at function definition time.

4. **Return early**: If you can determine the result early in the function, return immediately instead of using nested conditional statements.

5. **Use type hints**: For larger projects, consider using type hints to make your code more readable and catch type-related errors early:

```python
Copy
def greet(name: str) -> str:
    return f"Hello, {name}!"
```

1. **Test your functions**: Write unit tests for your functions to ensure they behave as expected.

Practical Examples

Let's look at some practical examples that demonstrate the concepts we've covered:

Example 1: Calculator Function

```python
Copy
def calculator(a, b, operation='add'):
    """

    Perform a calculation on two numbers.

    Args:
    a (float): The first number.
    b (float): The second number.
    operation (str): The operation
to perform (add, subtract,
 multiply, divide).

    Returns:
float: The result of the calculation.
    """
if operation == 'add':
        return a + b
    elif operation == '
```

```
      return a - b
elif operation == 'multiply':
       return a * b
elif operation == 'divide':
        if b != 0:
return a / b
       else:
return "Error: Division by zero"
    else:
return "Error: Invalid operation"

# Using the calculator function
print(calculator(5, 3))
 # Output: 8
print(calculator(5, 3,
'multiply'))  # Output: 15
print(calculator(5, 0,
'divide'))  # Output:
 Error: Division by zero
```

This example demonstrates:

- Default parameter values
- Return statements
- Error handling
- Docstrings

Example 2: Recursive Fibonacci Function

```python
Copy
def fibonacci(n):
    """

Calculate the nth Fibonacci
number recursively.
```

```
    Args:
    n (int): The position in
the Fibonacci sequence.

    Returns:
int: The nth Fibonacci number.
    """
    if n <= 1:
return n
    else:
return fibonacci(n-1) +
 fibonacci(n-2)

# Print the first 10
 Fibonacci numbers
for i in range(10):
    print(fibonacci(i), end=' ')
# Output:
 0 1 1 2 3 5 8 13 21 34
```

This example shows:

- Recursive function calls
- Using a function within a loop

Example 3: Higher-Order Function

```
python
Copy
def apply_operation(func, *args):
    """

Apply a function to a
 list of arguments.

    Args:
func (function):
```

```
The function to apply.
*args: Variable length argument list.

    Returns:
The result of applying the
 function to the arguments.
    """
    return func(*args)

def sum_squares(*numbers):
    return sum(x**2
for x in numbers)

result = apply_operation
(sum_squares, 1, 2, 3, 4)
print(result)  # Output: 30
```

This example demonstrates:

- Higher-order functions (functions that take other functions as arguments)
- Arbitrary number of arguments
- Lambda functions and list comprehensions

Conclusion

Functions are a powerful tool in Python that allow you to write more organized, reusable, and maintainable code. By mastering function definition, parameters, return values, and understanding variable scope, you'll be able to create more complex and efficient Python programs.

Remember that becoming proficient with functions takes practice. Try to identify repetitive code in your programs and think about how you can turn it into functions. As you gain experience, you'll develop an intuition for when and how to best use functions in your code.

In the next chapter, we'll explore Python's data structures in more depth, which will allow you to organize and manipulate data more effectively in your programs.

Chapter 5: Data Structures: Lists and Tuples

D
ata structures are fundamental components in programming that allow us to organize and manipulate data efficiently. In this chapter, we'll focus on two of Python's built-in data structures: lists and tuples. We'll explore how to create and manipulate these structures, dive into the power of list comprehensions, and understand the unique characteristics and uses of tuples.

Lists

Lists are one of the most versatile and commonly used data structures in Python. They are ordered, mutable sequences that can hold elements of different types.

Creating Lists

You can create a list by enclosing a comma-separated sequence of elements in square brackets:

```python
Copy
fruits = ["apple",
"banana", "cherry"]
```

```
mixed_list = [1,
"hello", 3.14, True]
```

You can also create an empty list and add elements to it later:

```python
Copy
empty_list = []
another_empty_list =
list()  # Using the list
() constructor
```

Accessing List Elements

List elements are indexed starting from 0. You can access individual elements using their index:

```python
Copy
fruits = ["apple",
  "banana", "cherry"]
print(fruits[0])
 # Output: apple
print(fruits[2])
 # Output: cherry
```

Python also supports negative indexing, where -1 refers to the last element:

```python
Copy
print(fruits[-1])
 # Output: cherry
print(fruits[-2])
   # Output: banana
```

Slicing Lists

You can extract a portion of a list using slicing:

```python
Copy
numbers = [0, 1, 2, 3, 4, 5]
print(numbers[2:5])
 # Output: [2, 3, 4]
print(numbers[:3])
  # Output: [0, 1, 2]
print(numbers[3:])
 # Output: [3, 4, 5]
print(numbers[::2])
 # Output: [0, 2, 4]
```

Modifying Lists

Lists are mutable, meaning you can change their content:

```python
Copy
fruits = ["apple",
 "banana", "cherry"]
fruits[1] = "blueberry"
print(fruits)  # Output:
 ['apple', 'blueberry
', 'cherry']
```

List Methods

Python provides several built-in methods for manipulating lists:

1. append(): Add an element to the end of the list

```python
Copy
fruits.append("date")
```

1. extend(): Add all elements from another iterable to the list

```python
Copy
more_fruits = ["elderberry", "fig"]
fruits.extend(more_fruits)
```

1. insert(): Insert an element at a specific position

```python
Copy
fruits.insert(1, "apricot")
```

1. remove(): Remove the first occurrence of a specific element

```python
Copy
fruits.remove("cherry")
```

1. pop(): Remove and return an element at a specific index (or the last element if no index is specified)

```python
Copy
last_fruit = fruits.pop()
second_fruit = fruits.pop(1)
```

1. index(): Return the index of the first occurrence of a specific element

```python
Copy
banana_index = fruits.
index("banana")
```

1. count(): Count the number of occurrences of a specific element

```python
Copy
apple_count =
fruits.count("apple")
```

1. sort(): Sort the list in-place

```python
Copy
fruits.sort()
```

1. reverse(): Reverse the order of elements in-place

```python
Copy
fruits.reverse()
```

List Operations

Lists support various operations:

1. Concatenation: Combine two lists using the + operator

```python
Copy
list1 = [1, 2, 3]
list2 = [4, 5, 6]
combined = list1 + list2
```

1. Repetition: Repeat a list using the * operator

```python
Copy
repeated = [1, 2]
* 3  # [1, 2, 1, 2, 1, 2]
```

1. Membership testing: Check if an element is in a list using the in operator

```python
Copy
```

```
if "apple" in fruits:
    print("We have apples!")
```

Nested Lists

Lists can contain other lists, creating multi-dimensional structures:

```python
Copy
matrix = [
    [1, 2, 3],
    [4, 5, 6],
    [7, 8, 9]
]
print(matrix[1][1])  # Output: 5
```

List Comprehensions

List comprehensions provide a concise way to create lists based on existing lists or other iterable objects. They combine the functionality of a loop and a conditional statement into a single line of code.

Basic Syntax

The basic syntax of a list comprehension is:

```python
Copy
new_list = [expression for item
in iterable if condition]
```

Here's a simple example that creates a list of squares:

```python
Copy
squares = [x**2 for x in range(10)]
print(squares)  # Output:
 [0, 1, 4, 9, 16,
 25, 36, 49, 64, 81]
```

List Comprehension with Conditional Logic

You can include conditional logic in list comprehensions:

```python
Copy
even_squares = [x**2 for
x in range(10)
if x % 2 == 0]
print(even_squares)
# Output:
[0, 4, 16, 36, 64]
```

Nested List Comprehensions

You can use nested list comprehensions to create more complex structures:

```python
Copy
matrix = [[i*j for j
 in range(1, 4)]
 for i in range(1, 4)]
print(matrix)
 # Output:
[[1, 2, 3],
 [2, 4, 6],
 [3, 6, 9]]
```

Advantages of List Comprehensions

1. Conciseness: List comprehensions often require less code than equivalent for loops.
2. Readability: Once you're familiar with the syntax, list comprehensions can be easier to read at a glance.
3. Performance: In many cases, list comprehensions are faster than equivalent for loops.

However, for very complex operations or when readability suffers, it's often better to use a traditional for loop.

Tuples

Tuples are similar to lists, but they are immutable, meaning their contents cannot be changed after creation. Tuples are often used to represent fixed collections of items.

Creating Tuples

You can create a tuple by enclosing a comma-separated sequence of elements in parentheses:

```python
Copy
coordinates = (3, 4)
person =
("Alice", 30, "New York")
```

You can also create a tuple without parentheses, known as tuple packing:

```python
Copy
```

```
coordinates = 3, 4
```

To create a tuple with a single element, you need to include a trailing comma:

```python
Copy
single_element_tuple = (42,)
```

Accessing Tuple Elements

Like lists, tuple elements are accessed using indexing:

```python
Copy
print(coordinates[0])
 # Output: 3
print(person[-1])
   # Output: New York
```

Tuple Unpacking

Tuple unpacking allows you to assign the elements of a tuple to individual variables:

```python
Copy
x, y = coordinates
name, age, city = person
```

This feature is particularly useful when a function returns multiple values:

```python
Copy
def get_user_info():
    return "Bob", 25, "Chicago"

name, age, city = get_user_info()
```

Tuple Methods

Tuples have only two built-in methods:

1. count(): Count the number of occurrences of a specific element

```python
Copy
numbers = (1, 2, 2, 3, 2, 4)
print(numbers.count(2))
  # Output: 3
```

1. index(): Return the index of the first occurrence of a specific element

```python
Copy
print(numbers.index(3))
  # Output: 3
```

Advantages of Tuples

1. Immutability: Once created, tuples cannot be modified. This makes them useful for representing data that shouldn't change.
2. Performance: In some cases, tuples can be more memory-efficient and

faster than lists.

3. Use as dictionary keys: Unlike lists, tuples can be used as keys in dictionaries because they are immutable.

Common Uses of Tuples

1. Returning multiple values from a function:

```python
Copy
def get_dimensions():
return 1920, 1080

width, height = get_dimensions()
```

1. Representing fixed data structures:

```python
Copy
chess_move =
('e', 2, 'e', 4)
```

1. As dictionary keys:

```python
Copy
locations = {
(40.7128, 74.0060):
 "New York City",
(51.5074, 0.1278): "London"
```

```
}
```

1. Multiple assignment:

```python
Copy
x, y, z = 1, 2, 3
```

Practical Examples

Let's look at some practical examples that demonstrate the concepts we've covered:

Example 1: Temperature Conversion

This example uses a list comprehension to convert temperatures from Celsius to Fahrenheit:

```python
Copy
celsius_temps = [0, 10,
  20, 30, 40]
fahrenheit_temps =
[(c * 9/5) + 32 for c
in celsius_temps]
print(fahrenheit_temps)
# Output: [32.0, 50.0,
  68.0, 86.0, 104.0]

# Creating a list of tuples
  with both Celsius and Fahrenheit temperatures
temp_pairs = [(c,
```

```python
(c * 9/5) + 32)
for c in celsius_temps]
print(temp_pairs)
 # Output: [(0, 32.0),
 (10, 50.0), (20, 68.0),
(30, 86.0), (40, 104.0)]

# Unpacking the tuples
to print a formatted output
for celsius, fahrenheit
in temp_pairs:
print(f"{celsius}
°C is equal to {fahrenheit}°F")
```

This example demonstrates:

- List comprehensions
- Creating tuples
- Tuple unpacking in a for loop

Example 2: Filtering and Transforming Data

This example shows how to use list comprehensions to filter and transform data:

```python
python
Copy
# List of dictionaries containing student information
students = [
{"name": "Alice", "age":
 20, "grade": 85},
{"name": "Bob",
"age": 22, "grade": 91},
{"name": "Charlie",
 "age": 21, "grade": 78},
{"name": "David",
```

```
"age": 20, "grade": 88}
]

# Get names of students with grade above 80
high_performers =
[student["name"]
for student in students if
student["grade"] > 80]
print("High performers:",
 high_performers)

# Create tuples of (name, age)
 for students aged 21 and above
older_students = [(student["name"],
student["age"]) for student in
students if student["age"] >= 21]
print("Students 21 and older:
", older_students)

# Calculate average grade
average_grade = sum(student["grade"]
for student in students) / len(students)
print(f"Average grade:
 {average_grade:.2f}")
```

This example shows:

- Complex list comprehensions with filtering
- Creating tuples within a list comprehension
- Using a generator expression (similar to a list comprehension) in the sum() function

Example 3: Working with Nested Structures

This example demonstrates working with nested lists and tuples:

```python
Copy
# Nested list representing a tic-tac-toe board
board = [
['X', 'O', 'X'],
['O', 'X', 'O'],
['O', 'X', 'X']
]


# Function to check if a player has won
def check_win(player):
    # Check rows
    for row in board:
if all(cell == player for cell in row):
return True

    # Check columns
    for col in range(3):
if all(board[row][col]
 == player for row in range(3)):
            return True

    # Check diagonals
    if all(board[i][i] ==
player for i in range(3)):
        return True
if all(board[i][2-i]
== player for i in range(3)):
        return True

    return False

# Check if 'X' or 'O' has won
for player in ('X', 'O'):
    if check_win(player):
print(f"Player {player} has won!")

# Flatten the board into a single list
flat_board = [cell for
row in board for cell in row]
```

```
print("Flattened board:", flat_board)

# Count the number of 'X's and 'O's
x_count = flat_board.count('X')
o_count = flat_board.count('O')
print(f"X count: {x_count},
 O count: {o_count}")
```

This example demonstrates:

- Working with nested lists
- Using list comprehensions with nested loops
- Using tuples to represent fixed data (players)
- Flattening a nested list structure

Conclusion

Lists and tuples are fundamental data structures in Python that allow you to organize and manipulate collections of data efficiently. Lists offer flexibility with their mutability and wide range of built-in methods, while tuples provide immutability and are often used to represent fixed collections of items.

List comprehensions provide a powerful and concise way to create and transform lists, often leading to more readable and efficient code. However, it's important to balance their use with traditional loops when dealing with more complex logic.

As you continue your Python journey, you'll find that mastering these data structures and techniques will greatly enhance your ability to write efficient and expressive code. Practice working with lists and tuples in various scenarios, and don't hesitate to explore the Python documentation for more advanced usage and methods.

In the next chapter, we'll explore more complex data structures like dictionaries and sets, which will further expand your toolkit for organizing and manipulating data in Python.

Chapter 6: Dictionaries and Sets

In this chapter, we'll explore two more powerful data structures in Python: dictionaries and sets. These structures offer unique capabilities for organizing and manipulating data efficiently. We'll learn how to work with key-value pairs in dictionaries, perform set operations, and understand when to use dictionaries versus lists.

Dictionaries

Dictionaries are unordered collections of key-value pairs. They are also known as associative arrays, hash tables, or hash maps in other programming languages. Dictionaries are highly optimized for retrieving data when you know the key.

Creating Dictionaries

You can create a dictionary by enclosing a comma-separated list of key-value pairs in curly braces {}:

```python
Copy
person = {"name": "Alice",
"age": 30, "city":
  "New York"}
```

You can also use the dict() constructor:

```python
Copy
person = dict(name="Alice",
  age=30, city="New York")
```

Accessing Dictionary Values

You can access dictionary values using their keys:

```python
Copy
print(person["name"])
 # Output: Alice
```

If you try to access a key that doesn't exist, Python will raise a KeyError. To avoid this, you can use the get() method, which returns None (or a specified default value) if the key doesn't exist:

```python
Copy
print(person.get("name"))
    # Output: Alice
print(person.get("country"))
 # Output: None
print(person.get("country",
  "Unknown"))  # Output: Unknown
```

Modifying Dictionaries

Dictionaries are mutable, so you can add, modify, or remove key-value pairs:

```python
Copy
# Adding a new key-value pair
person["occupation"] = "Engineer"

# Modifying an existing value
person["age"] = 31

# Removing a key-value pair
del person["city"]
```

Dictionary Methods

Python provides several useful methods for working with dictionaries:

1. keys(): Returns a view of the dictionary's keys

```python
Copy
print(person.keys())
```

1. values(): Returns a view of the dictionary's values

```python
Copy
print(person.values())
```

1. items(): Returns a view of the dictionary's key-value pairs as tuples

```python
Copy
print(person.items())
```

1. update(): Updates the dictionary with elements from another dictionary or iterable of key-value pairs

```python
Copy
person.update({"city":
"San Francisco", "hobbies":
["reading", "hiking"]})
```

1. pop(): Removes and returns the value for a specified key

```python
Copy
age = person.pop("age")
```

1. popitem(): Removes and returns an arbitrary key-value pair as a tuple

```python
Copy
last_item = person.popitem()
```

1. clear(): Removes all items from the dictionary

```python
Copy
person.clear()
```

Dictionary Comprehensions

Similar to list comprehensions, Python supports dictionary comprehensions:

```python
Copy
squares = {x: x**2 for x in range(6)}
print(squares)  # Output:
 {0: 0, 1: 1, 2:
 4, 3: 9, 4:
16, 5: 25}
```

Nested Dictionaries

Dictionaries can contain other dictionaries, allowing you to create complex, nested data structures:

```python
Copy
users = {
"Alice": {"age": 30,
 "occupation": "Engineer"},
"Bob": {"age": 25,
 "occupation": "Designer"}
}

print(users["Alice"
]["occupation"])
```

```
# Output: Engineer
```

Sets

Sets are unordered collections of unique elements. They are useful for membership testing, removing duplicates from sequences, and performing mathematical set operations.

Creating Sets

You can create a set by enclosing a comma-separated sequence of elements in curly braces {}:

```python
Copy
fruits = {"apple",
"banana", "cherry"}
```

You can also use the set() constructor:

```python
Copy
numbers = set([1, 2, 2, 3, 4, 4, 5])
print(numbers)  # Output:
  {1, 2, 3, 4, 5}
```

Note that duplicate elements are automatically removed.

Set Operations

Sets support various mathematical operations:

1. Union: Combine elements from two sets (removing duplicates)

```python
Copy
set1 = {1, 2, 3}
set2 = {3, 4, 5}
union_set = set1
| set2  # or set1.union(set2)
print(union_set)
 # Output: {1, 2, 3, 4, 5}
```

1. Intersection: Get elements common to both sets

```python
Copy
intersection_set = set1 & set2
 # or set1.intersection(set2)
print(intersection_set)
 # Output: {3}
```

1. Difference: Get elements in one set but not in the other

```python
Copy
difference_set = set1 - set2
 # or set1.difference(set2)
print(difference_set)
 # Output: {1, 2}
```

1. Symmetric Difference: Get elements in either set, but not in both

```python
Copy
symmetric_difference =
set1 ^ set2  # or set1.
symmetric_difference(set2)
print(symmetric_difference)
  # Output: {1, 2, 4, 5}
```

Set Methods

Sets provide several methods for manipulation:

1. add(): Add an element to the set

```python
Copy
fruits.add("date")
```

1. remove(): Remove a specified element (raises KeyError if not found)

```python
Copy
fruits.remove("banana")
```

1. discard(): Remove a specified element if it exists (no error if not found)

```python
Copy
fruits.discard("grape")
```

1. pop(): Remove and return an arbitrary element

```python
Copy
removed_fruit = fruits.pop()
```

1. clear(): Remove all elements from the set

```python
Copy
fruits.clear()
```

Set Comprehensions

Like lists and dictionaries, Python supports set comprehensions:

```python
Copy
even_squares = {x**2 for x in range(10)
if x % 2 == 0}
print(even_squares)
# Output: {0, 4, 16, 36, 64}
```

When to Use Dictionaries vs. Lists

Choosing between dictionaries and lists depends on your specific use case. Here are some guidelines:

Use Dictionaries When:

1. You need key-value associations

- Example: Storing user information where the username is the key

```python
Copy
users = {"alice": {"email":
"alice@example.com", "age": 30},
"bob": {"email":
"bob@example.com", "age": 25}}
```

1. You need fast lookup by key

- Dictionaries have O(1) average time complexity for key lookup

1. You want to represent structured data

- Example: Representing a configuration with named parameters

```python
Copy
config = {"host": "localhost",
 "port": 8080, "debug": True}
```

1. You need to count occurrences of items

- Example: Counting word frequencies in a text

```python
Copy
word_counts = {}
for word in text.split():
    word_counts[word] =
 word_counts.get(word, 0) + 1
```

1. You want to associate additional data with objects

- Example: Caching computation results

```python
Copy
factorial_cache = {}
def factorial(n):
    if n in factorial_cache:
return factorial_cache[n]
    result = 1
    for i in range(1, n+1):
        result *= i
factorial_cache[n] = result
    return result
```

Use Lists When:

1. You need ordered data

- Lists maintain the order of elements as inserted

1. You need to store duplicate elements

- Lists allow duplicate elements, while dictionary keys and set elements must be unique

1. You need to perform operations on a sequence of elements

- Example: Calculating the sum or average of numbers

```python
Copy
numbers = [1, 2, 3, 4, 5]
average = sum(numbers)
/ len(numbers)
```

1. You need to access elements by index

- Lists support integer indexing and slicing

1. You want to represent a collection of similar items

- Example: A list of tasks or a sequence of events

```python
Copy
tasks = ["Buy groceries",
  "Clean house", "Do laundry"]
```

Practical Examples

Let's look at some practical examples that demonstrate the concepts we've covered:

Example 1: Word Frequency Counter

This example uses a dictionary to count word frequencies in a text:

```python
Copy
def word_frequency(text):
    # Convert text to lowercase
and split into words
    words = text.lower().split()

    # Count word frequencies using a dictionary
frequency = {}
for word in words:
frequency[word] =
 frequency.get(word, 0) + 1

# Sort the dictionary by value
 (frequency) in descending order
sorted_frequency =
sorted(frequency.items(),
 key=lambda x: x[1],
reverse=True)

return dict(sorted_frequency)

# Example usage
text = "The quick brown fox
 jumps over the lazy dog. T
he dog barks, and the
fox runs away."
result = word_frequency(text)
```

```
# Print the top 5 most
frequent words
for word, count in list
(result.items())[:5]:
print(f"{word}: {count}")
```

This example demonstrates:

- Using a dictionary to count occurrences
- The get() method with a default value
- Sorting a dictionary by value
- Dictionary comprehension (when converting back to a dict)

Example 2: Student Grade Tracker

This example uses nested dictionaries and sets to manage student grades:

```python
Copy
class GradeTracker:
    def __init__(self):
        self.students = {}

def add_grade(self,
student, subject, grade):
if student not in self.students:
self.students[student] = {}
self.students[student][subject] = grade

def get_average(self, student):
if student in self.students:
grades = self.
students[student].values()
return sum(grades)
/ len(grades)
return None
```

```python
def get_top_subject(self, student):
if student in self.students:
return max(self.students[student],
 key=self.students[student].get)
return None

def get_all_subjects(self):
subjects = set()
for student_grades in self.
students.values():
subjects.update
(student_grades.keys())
return subjects

# Example usage
tracker = GradeTracker()

tracker.add_grade
("Alice", "Math", 85)
tracker.add_grade
("Alice", "Science", 92)
tracker.add_grade
("Alice", "History", 78)
tracker.add_grade(
"Bob", "Math", 91)
tracker.add_grade
("Bob", "Science", 82)
tracker.add_grade
("Charlie", "Math", 76)
tracker.add_grade
("Charlie", "Science", 89)
tracker.add_grade(
"Charlie", "English", 95)

print(f"Alice's average grade:
 {tracker.get_average
('Alice'):.2f}")
print(f"Bob's top subject:
 {tracker.get_top_subject
```

```
('Bob')}")
print(f"All subjects:
{', '.join(tracker.
get_all_subjects())}")
```

This example demonstrates:

- Using nested dictionaries to store student grades
- Calculating averages using dictionary values
- Finding the key with the maximum value in a dictionary
- Using a set to collect unique subjects across all students

Example 3: Recipe Ingredient Scaling

This example uses dictionaries and sets to scale recipe ingredients:

```python
Copy
def scale_recipe(recipe,
servings, target_servings):
scaling_factor =
target_servings / servings
scaled_recipe = {}

for ingredient,
amount in recipe.items():
scaled_recipe[ingredient]
 = amount * scaling_factor

    return scaled_recipe

def combine_recipes(recipe1, recipe2):
combined = recipe1.copy()
for ingredient, amount
in recipe2.items():
combined[ingredient] =
```

```python
combined.get(ingredient, 0)
 + amount
    return combined

# Example recipes
pancakes = {
"flour": 2,   # cups
"milk": 1.5,   # cups
"eggs": 2,
"butter": 2,
 # tablespoons
"sugar": 2,
 # tablespoons
}

waffles = {
"flour": 1.75,   # cups
"milk": 1.5,   # cups
"eggs": 2,
"butter": 4,   # tablespoons
"sugar": 1,   # tablespoon
"baking powder": 1,
   # tablespoon
}

# Scale pancake recipe for 6 servings
 (original is for 4)
scaled_pancakes =
scale_recipe(pancakes, 4, 6)
print("Scaled Pancake Recipe
 (6 servings):")
for ingredient, amount in
scaled_pancakes.items():
print(f"{ingredient}:
{amount:.2f}")

# Combine pancake and waffle recipes
combined_recipe = combine_
recipes(pancakes, waffles)
print("\nCombined Recipe:")
```

```
for ingredient, amount in
combined_recipe.items():
print(f"{ingredient}: {amount:.2f}")

# Find unique ingredients using sets
pancake_ingredients =
 set(pancakes.keys())
waffle_ingredients =
set(waffles.keys())

unique_to_pancakes =
pancake_ingredients -
waffle_ingredients
unique_to_waffles =
waffle_ingredients -
 pancake_ingredients

print("\nIngredients unique
to pancakes:", ",
".join(unique_to_pancakes))
print("Ingredients
unique to waffles:
", ", ".join(unique_to_waffles))
```

This example demonstrates:

- Using dictionaries to represent recipes
- Scaling recipe ingredients using dictionary operations
- Combining recipes by adding ingredient amounts
- Using sets to find unique ingredients in each recipe

Conclusion

Dictionaries and sets are powerful data structures in Python that offer unique capabilities for organizing and manipulating data. Dictionaries provide fast key-value lookups and are ideal for representing structured data, while sets are perfect for managing collections of unique elements and performing mathematical set operations.

Understanding when to use dictionaries versus lists is crucial for writing efficient and readable code. Generally, use dictionaries when you need key-value associations or fast lookups, and use lists when you need ordered sequences of elements or want to maintain duplicates.

As you continue your Python journey, you'll find that mastering these data structures will greatly enhance your ability to solve complex problems efficiently. Practice working with dictionaries and sets in various scenarios, and don't hesitate to explore the Python documentation for more advanced usage and methods.

In the next chapter, we'll explore file handling and input/output operations, which will allow you to work with external data and persist your program's results.

Chapter 7: File Handling and Input/Output

I n this chapter, we'll explore how to work with files and handle input/output operations in Python. We'll cover reading from and writing to files, working with CSV and JSON formats, and handling user input. These skills are essential for processing data, storing information, and creating interactive programs.

Reading from and Writing to Files

Python provides built-in functions and methods for working with files. The basic process involves opening a file, performing read or write operations, and then closing the file.

Opening and Closing Files

To open a file, use the open() function:

```python
Copy
file = open('example.txt',
 'r')  # 'r' mode for reading
# Perform operations with the file
file.close()
```

```
# Close the file when done
```

It's important to close files after you're done with them to free up system resources. A better practice is to use a with statement, which automatically closes the file:

```python
Copy
with open('example.txt', 'r') as file:
# Perform operations with the file
# File is automatically closed when the block ends
```

Common file modes include:

- 'r': Read (default)
- 'w': Write (creates a new file or truncates an existing file)
- 'a': Append (adds to the end of the file)
- 'r+': Read and write
- 'b': Binary mode (used with other modes like 'rb' or 'wb')

Reading from Files

There are several methods to read from files:

1. read(): Reads the entire file content

```python
Copy
with open('example.txt',
 'r') as file:
content = file.read()
print(content)
```

1. readline(): Reads one line at a time

```python
Copy
with open('example.txt'
, 'r') as file:
line = file.readline()
while line:
print(line, end='')
line = file.readline()
```

1. readlines(): Reads all lines into a list

```python
Copy
with open('example.txt',
 'r') as file:
lines = file.readlines()
for line in lines:
print(line, end='')
```

1. Iterating over the file object:

```python
Copy
with open('example.txt',
 'r') as file:
for line in file:
print(line, end='')
```

Writing to Files

To write to files, use the write() method:

```python
Copy
with open('output.txt',
 'w') as file:
  file.write("Hello, World!\n")
file.write
("This is a new line.")
```

For writing multiple lines, you can use writelines():

```python
Copy
lines = ["Line 1\n",
 "Line 2\n", "Line 3\n"]
with open('output.
txt', 'w') as file:
file.writelines(lines)
```

Appending to Files

To add content to the end of an existing file, use the append mode:

```python
Copy
with open('log.txt',
 'a') as file:
file.write
("New log entry\n")
```

Working with Binary Files

For non-text files (like images), use binary mode:

```python
Copy
# Reading a binary file
with open('image.jpg',
 'rb') as file:
image_data = file.read()

# Writing to a binary file
with open('copy_image.
jpg', 'wb') as file:
file.write(image_data)
```

Working with CSV Files

CSV (Comma-Separated Values) is a common format for storing tabular data. Python's csv module provides functionality for reading from and writing to CSV files.

Reading CSV Files

To read a CSV file:

```python
Copy
import csv

with open('data.csv', 'r') as file:
csv_reader = csv.reader(file)
for row in csv_reader:
print(row)
```

For CSV files with headers, you can use csv.DictReader:

```python
Copy
with open('data.csv',
 'r') as file:
csv_reader = csv.DictReader(file)
for row in csv_reader:
print(row['column_name'])
```

Writing CSV Files

To write to a CSV file:

```python
Copy
import csv

data = [
['Name', 'Age', 'City'],
['Alice', '30', 'New York'],
['Bob', '25',
 'Los Angeles']
]

with open('output.
csv', 'w', newline='')
 as file:
csv_writer =
csv.writer(file)
csv_writer.
writerows(data)
```

To write dictionaries to a CSV file:

```python
Copy
data = [
    {'Name': 'Alice',
 'Age': '30', 'City':
'New York'},
    {'Name': 'Bob',
'Age': '25', 'City':
 'Los Angeles'}
]

with open('output.csv',
'w', newline='') as file:
fieldnames =
['Name', 'Age', 'City']
csv_writer =
csv.DictWriter
(file, fieldnames=fieldnames)


csv_writer.writeheader()

csv_writer.writerows(data)
```

Working with JSON Files

JSON (JavaScript Object Notation) is a lightweight data interchange format. Python's json module provides methods for encoding and decoding JSON data.

Reading JSON Files

To read a JSON file:

```
python
Copy
import json

with open('data.json',
 'r') as file:
data = json.load(file)
print(data)
```

Writing JSON Files

To write to a JSON file:

```
python
Copy
import json

data = {
"name": "Alice",
"age": 30,
"city": "New York"
}

with open('output.j
son', 'w') as file:
json.dump(data,
file, indent=4)
```

The indent parameter is optional and makes the output more readable.

Working with JSON Strings

You can also work with JSON strings using json.loads() and json.dumps():

```python
Copy
import json

# JSON string to Python object
json_string = '
{"name": "Bob", "age": 25}'
python_obj = j
son.loads(json_string)
print(python_obj['name'])

# Python object
to JSON string
python_obj =
 {"name": "Charlie",
 "age": 35}
json_string = json.
dumps(python_obj)
print(json_string)
```

Handling User Input

Python provides several ways to handle user input, allowing you to create interactive programs.

Basic Input

The input() function reads a line of text from the user:

```python
Copy
name = input
("Enter your name: ")
print(f"Hello, {name}!")
```

Handling Different Types of Input

By default, input() returns a string. To get other types, you need to convert the input:

```python
Copy
age = int(input
("Enter your age: "))
height = float(input(
"Enter your height
  in meters: "))
```

Be sure to handle potential ValueErrors when converting input:

```python
Copy
try:
age = int(input
("Enter your age: "))
except ValueError:
print("Please enter
a valid integer for age.")
```

Creating a Simple Menu

You can create a simple menu system using a loop and conditional statements:

```python
Copy
while True:
print("\nMenu:")
print("1. Say hello")
print("2. Calculate
```

```
  age in dog years")
print("3. Exit")

choice = input
("Enter your choice (1-3): ")

if choice == '1':
name = input("Enter your name: ")
print(f"Hello, {name}!")
    elif choice == '2':
        try:
age = int(input
("Enter your age: "))
dog_age = age * 7
print(f"Your age in dog years is: {dog_age}")
except ValueError:
print("Please
enter a valid integer for age.")
elif choice == '3':
print("Goodbye!")
break
    else:
print("Invalid choice.
 Please try again.")
```

Practical Examples

Let's look at some practical examples that demonstrate the concepts we've covered:

Example 1: Log File Analyzer

This example reads a log file, analyzes its contents, and writes a summary to a new file:

```python
Copy
import re
from collections import Counter

def analyze_log
(input_file, output_file):
    ip_pattern =
r'\d{1,3}\.\d{1,3}\.
\d{1,3}\.\d{1,3}'
ip_addresses = []

with open(input_
file, 'r') as file:
for line in file:
match = re.search
(ip_pattern, line)
if match:
ip_addresses.
append(match.group())

ip_counts =
Counter(ip_addresses)

with open
(output_file, 'w') as file:
file.write("Log
 Analysis Summary\n")
file.write("====
==========
======\n\n")
file.write(f"Total
 IP addresses found: {len(ip_addresses)}\n")
file.write(f"Unique IP addresses: {len(ip_counts)}\n\n")
file.write("Top
5 IP addresses:\n")
for ip, count in ip_
counts.most_common(5):
file.write(f"{ip}:
{count} times\n")
```

```
# Usage
analyze_log('server.log', 'log_summary.txt')
print("Analysis complete.
Results written to
 log_summary.txt")
```

This example demonstrates:

- Reading from and writing to text files
- Using regular expressions to extract information
- Using the collections.Counter class for counting occurrences

Example 2: CSV Data Processor

This example reads data from a CSV file, processes it, and writes the results to a new CSV file:

```python
python
Copy
import csv
from datetime import datetime

def process_sales_data(input_file, output_file):
    sales_by_month = {}

    with open(input_file,
'r') as file:
csv_reader = csv.
DictReader(file)
for row in csv_reader:
date = datetime.
strptime(row['Date'],
'%Y-%m-%d')
month = date.
strftime('%Y-%m')
amount = float(row['Amount'])
```

```
if month in sales_by_month:
sales_by_month[month]
+= amount
            else:
sales_by_month
[month] = amount

    with open(output_
file, 'w', newline='') as file:
csv_writer = csv.writer(file)
csv_writer.writerow
(['Month', 'Total Sales'])

for month, total in sorted(sales_
by_month.items()):
csv_writer.writerow([month, f"{total:.2f}"])

# Usage
process_sales_data('sales.csv', 'monthly_sales.csv')
print("Processing
complete. Results written to monthly_sales.csv")
```

This example demonstrates:

- Reading from and writing to CSV files
- Processing data using dictionaries
- Working with dates and times

Example 3: JSON Configuration Manager

This example creates a simple configuration manager that reads and writes settings to a JSON file:

```
python
Copy
```

```python
import json

class ConfigManager:
def __init__
(self, filename):
self.filename = filename
self.config = {}
self.load_config()

    def load_config(self):
try:
with open(self.
filename, 'r') as file:
self.config =
json.load(file)
except FileNotFoundError:
print(f"Config file
{self.filename} not found.
 Starting with
empty configuration.")

def save_config(self):
with open(self.
filename, 'w') as file:
json.dump(self.
config, file, indent=4)

def get(self, key,
 default=None):
return self.config.
get(key, default)

def set(self, key, value):
 self.config[key] = value
  self.save_config()

    def delete(self, key):
if key in self.config:
del self.config[key]
self.save_config()
```

101

```python
# Usage
config = ConfigManager
('app_config.json')

# Set some configuration values
config.set('debug_mode', True)
config.set('max_connections', 100)

# Read configuration values
print(f"Debug mode:
{config.get
('debug_mode')}")
print(f"Max connections:
 {config.get
('max_connections')}")

# Delete a configuration value
config.delete
('max_connections')

print("Configuration saved to app_config.json")
```

This example demonstrates:

- Reading from and writing to JSON files
- Creating a class to manage configuration data
- Handling file not found errors

Example 4: Interactive Quiz Game

This example creates a simple quiz game that reads questions from a file and handles user input:

```python
python
Copy
```

```python
import json
import random

def load_questions(filename):
with open(filename,
 'r') as file:
return json.load(file)

def run_quiz(questions):
    score = 0
total = len(questions)

    for question in random.sample
(questions, total):
print(
"\n" + question['question'])
for i, option in enumerate
(question[
'options'], 1):
print(f"{i}. {option}")

while True:
try:
answer = int
(input("Enter your
 answer (1-4): "))
if 1 <= answer <= 4:
break
else:
print("Please enter
a number between 1 and 4.")
except ValueError:
print("Please enter
 a valid number.")

if question
['options'][answer-1] == question['correct_answer']:
print("Correct!")
score += 1
else:
```

```
print(f"Sorry,
the correct answer was:
{question['correct
_answer']}")

print(f"\nQuiz
complete! Your score:
 {score}/{total}")

# Main program
questions = load_questions
('quiz_questions.json')
print("Welcome
to the Python Quiz Game!")
run_quiz(questions)
```

This example demonstrates:

- Reading data from a JSON file
- Handling user input with error checking
- Creating an interactive program structure

Conclusion

File handling and input/output operations are crucial skills for any Python programmer. They allow you to work with external data, persist information, and create interactive programs. We've covered reading from and writing to files, working with CSV and JSON formats, and handling user input.

Remember to always close files after you're done with them, or better yet, use the with statement to automatically manage file resources. When working with user input, always validate and sanitize the input to ensure your program behaves correctly and securely.

As you continue your Python journey, you'll find these skills invaluable for data processing, configuration management, and creating more complex applications. Practice working with different file formats and creating interactive programs to reinforce your understanding of these concepts.

In the next chapter, we'll explore error handling and debugging techniques, which will help you write more robust and reliable Python programs.

Chapter 8: Error Handling and Debugging

I

n this chapter, we'll explore error handling and debugging techniques in Python. These skills are crucial for writing robust, reliable code and for efficiently identifying and fixing issues in your programs. We'll cover try-except blocks, common exceptions and how to handle them, and various debugging techniques.

Try-Except Blocks

Try-except blocks are the primary mechanism for handling exceptions (errors) in Python. They allow you to gracefully handle errors that might occur during program execution.

Basic Syntax

The basic syntax of a try-except block is as follows:

```python
Copy
try:
# Code that might
raise an exception
result = 10 / 0
except ZeroDivisionError:
# Code to handle the
  specific exception
```

```
print("Error:
Division by zero!")
```

Multiple Except Blocks

You can handle multiple exceptions using multiple except blocks:

```python
Copy
try:
number = int(input
("Enter a number: "))
result = 10 / number
except ValueError:
print("Error:
Please enter a valid number!")
except
ZeroDivisionError:
print("Error:
  Cannot divide by zero!")
```

Catching Multiple Exceptions

You can also catch multiple exceptions in a single except block:

```python
Copy
try:
    # Some code that might
  raise exceptions
except (ValueError,
 ZeroDivisionError) as e:
    print(f"An
error occurred: {e}")
```

The Else Clause

The else clause in a try-except block is executed if no exception is raised:

```python
Copy
try:
number = int(input
("Enter a number: "))
except ValueError:
print("That's not
 a valid number!")
else:
print(f"You entered
 {number}")
```

The Finally Clause

The finally clause is executed regardless of whether an exception was raised or not:

```python
Copy
try:
    file = open(
"example.txt", "r")
# Perform some operations
except FileNotFoundError:
print("The
 file was not found.")
finally:
file.close()
 # This will always execute
```

Creating Custom Exceptions

You can create your own exception classes by inheriting from the built-in
Exception class:

```python
Copy
class CustomError(Exception):
    pass

def validate_age(age):
if age < 0:
raise CustomError
("Age cannot be negative")

try:
validate_age(-5)
except CustomError as e:
print(f"CustomError: {e}")
```

Common Exceptions and How to Handle Them

Python has many built-in exceptions. Here are some of the most common
ones and how to handle them:

1. ValueError

Raised when a function receives an argument of the correct type but an
inappropriate value:

```python
Copy
try:
age = int(input
("Enter your age: "))
```

```
except ValueError:
print("Please enter
 a valid integer for age.")
```

2. TypeError

Raised when an operation or function is applied to an object of an inappropriate type:

```python
Copy
try:
    result = "5" + 5
except TypeError:
print("Cannot
add a string and an integer.")
```

3. IndexError

Raised when trying to access an index that is out of range:

```python
Copy
my_list = [1, 2, 3]
try:
print(my_list[3])
except IndexError:
print("Index
is out of range.")
```

4. KeyError

Raised when a dictionary key is not found:

```python
Copy
my_dict = {"a": 1, "b": 2}
try:
value = my_dict["c"]
except KeyError:
print
("Key not found
in the dictionary.")
```

5. FileNotFoundError

Raised when trying to open a file that doesn't exist:

```python
Copy
try:
with open("nonexistent
_file.txt", "r") as file:
content = file.read()
except FileNotFoundError:
print("The file does
not exist.")
```

6. ZeroDivisionError

Raised when dividing by zero:

```python
Copy
```

```
try:
result = 10 / 0
except ZeroDivisionError:
print("Cannot
divide by zero.")
```

7. AttributeError

Raised when an attribute reference or assignment fails:

```
python
Copy
class MyClass:
    pass

obj = MyClass()
try:
print(obj.nonexis
tent_attribute)
except AttributeError:
print("The attribute
does not exist.")
```

General Exception Handling

While it's generally better to catch specific exceptions, sometimes you might want to catch any exception:

```
python
Copy
try:
# Some code that
might raise various exceptions
```

```
except Exception as e:
print(f"An error
 occurred: {e}")
```

However, use this sparingly, as it can make debugging more difficult by catching unexpected errors.

Debugging Techniques

Debugging is the process of finding and fixing errors in your code. Python provides several tools and techniques to help with debugging.

1. Print Debugging

The simplest form of debugging is to use print statements to output variable values and program flow:

```python
python
Copy
def calculate_average(numbers):
print(f"Input: {numbers}")
  # Debug print
total = sum(numbers)
print(f"Total: {total}")
 # Debug print
count = len(numbers)
print(f"Count: {count}")
  # Debug print
return total / count

result = calculate_
average([1, 2, 3, 4, 5])
print(f"Result: {result}")
```

While simple, this method can be cumbersome for large programs and should be used sparingly in production code.

2. Using the assert Statement

The assert statement is used to ensure that a condition is true. If it's not, it raises an AssertionError:

```python
Copy
def divide(a, b):
assert b != 0,
"Divisor cannot be zero"
return a / b

try:
result = divide(10, 0)
except AssertionError as e:
print(f"AssertionError: {e}")
```

3. Using the Python Debugger (pdb)

Python's built-in debugger, pdb, allows you to step through your code line by line:

```python
Copy
import pdb

def complex_function(x, y):
result = x + y
pdb.set_trace()
 # Debugger will start here
for i in range(5):
result *= i
return result

complex_function(3, 4)
```

When the debugger starts, you can use commands like:

- n (next): Execute the next line
- s (step): Step into a function call
- c (continue): Continue execution until the next breakpoint
- p (print): Print the value of an expression
- q (quit): Quit the debugger

4. Using an Integrated Development Environment (IDE)

Most modern IDEs, like PyCharm, Visual Studio Code, or IDLE, come with built-in debuggers that provide a graphical interface for debugging. These often include features like:

- Breakpoints
- Step-by-step execution
- Variable inspection
- Call stack viewing

5. Logging

Python's logging module provides a flexible framework for generating log messages:

```python
Copy
import logging

logging.basicConfig
(level=logging.DEBUG)

def complex_
calculation(a, b):
logging.debug
(f"Inputs: a={a}, b={b}")
result = a * b
logging.debug
```

```
(f"Intermediate
result: {result}")
result += a - b
logging.debug
(f"Final result:
 {result}")
return result

complex_calculation(5, 3)
```

Logging is particularly useful for debugging issues in production environments where you can't use interactive debugging tools.

6. Using try-except with Logging

Combining exception handling with logging can provide valuable information for debugging:

```python
Copy
import logging

logging.basicConfig
(level=logging.
ERROR,
filename='app.log')

def divide(a, b):
    try:
result = a / b
except ZeroDivisionError:
logging.error
(f"Division by
zero attempted with
a={a} and b={b}")
raise
    return result
```

```
try:
    divide(10, 0)
except ZeroDivisionError:
print("Cannot divide by zero")
```

This approach logs the error details to a file, which can be reviewed later.

Best Practices for Error Handling and Debugging

1. **Be specific with exceptions**: Catch specific exceptions rather than using a broad except clause. This makes your code more robust and easier to debug.

2. **Use logging instead of print statements**: Logging provides more control over output and can be easily configured for different environments (development, production, etc.).

3. **Don't suppress exceptions**: Avoid empty except clauses. Always handle or re-raise exceptions.

4. **Use context managers**: Use with statements when working with resources like files to ensure they are properly closed, even if an exception occurs.

5. **Provide useful error messages**: When raising exceptions, include informative error messages to make debugging easier.

6. **Use debugger breakpoints strategically**: Place breakpoints at critical points in your code where you suspect issues might occur.

7. **Understand the call stack**: When an exception occurs, examine the full call stack to understand the sequence of function calls that led to the error.

8. **Use assertions for internal checks**: Use assert statements to check for conditions that should always be true in your code.

9. **Write unit tests**: Comprehensive unit tests can catch many errors before they make it into production code.

10. **Keep your code clean and well-organized**: Well-structured code is

easier to debug. Follow Python's style guide (PEP 8) and use meaningful variable and function names.

Practical Examples

Let's look at some practical examples that demonstrate error handling and debugging techniques:

Example 1: File Processing with Error Handling

This example reads a CSV file, processes its contents, and writes results to a new file, using error handling throughout:

```python
Copy
import csv
import logging

logging.basicConfig(level=logging.ERROR,
filename='data_processing.log')

def process_data
(input_file, output_file):
    try:
with open(input_file, 'r') as infile,
 open(output_file, 'w', newline='')
as outfile:
reader = csv.reader(infile)
writer = csv.writer(outfile)

header = next(reader)
writer.writerow(header + ['Total'])

for row in reader:
                try:
total = sum(float(value)
for value in row[1:])
```

```
writer.writerow(row +
[f"{total:.2f}"])
except ValueError as e:
logging.error(f"Error processing row
{reader.line_num}: {e}")
writer.writerow(row + ['ERROR'])

print(f"Data processed successfully.
 Results written to {output_file}")
    except FileNotFoundError:
logging.error(f"Input file
'{input_file}' not found.")
print(f"Error: Input file
'{input_file}' not found.")
    except PermissionError:
logging.error(f"Permission
denied when writing to
'{output_file}'")
print(f"Error:
 Permission denied when writing
 to '{output_file}'")
except Exception as e:
logging.error
(f"Unexpected error: {e}")
print(f"An unexpected
error occurred. Check the
log file for details.")

# Usage
process_data('input_data.csv',
'output_data.csv')
```

This example demonstrates:

- Using try-except blocks for file operations and data processing
- Logging errors to a file
- Handling specific exceptions (FileNotFoundError, PermissionError)
- Using a general Exception handler as a fallback

Example 2: Web Scraping with Debugging

This example scrapes a website for information, using debugging techniques to handle potential issues:

```python
Copy
import requests
from bs4 import BeautifulSoup
import logging
import pdb

logging.basicConfig(level=
logging.DEBUG, format='%(asctime)s
- %(levelname)s - %(message)s')

def scrape_website(url):
    try:
logging.info(f"Attempting to scrape {url}")
response = requests.get(url)
response.raise_for_status()
# Raises an HTTPError for bad responses

soup = BeautifulSoup
(response.text, 'html.parser')

# Example: Extract all paragraph texts
paragraphs = soup.find_all('p')

        if not paragraphs:
logging.warning
("No paragraphs found on the page")
pdb.set_trace()
 # Start debugger if no paragraphs are found

for i, p in enumerate(paragraphs):
logging.debug(f"Paragraph
 {i + 1}: {p.text[:50]}...")
 # Log first 50 chars of each paragraph
```

```
return [p.text for p in paragraphs]

except requests.exceptions.
RequestException as e:
logging.error
(f"Error fetching the website: {e}")
except Exception as e:
logging.error
(f"Unexpected error: {e}")
pdb.post_mortem()
# Start post-mortem debugging on exception

# Usage
url = "https://example.com"
results = scrape_website(url)

if results:
print(f"Successfully scraped
 {len(results)} paragraphs from {url}")
else:
    print("Scraping failed.
 Check the log for details.")
```

This example demonstrates:

- Using logging for different levels of messages (info, debug, warning, error)
- Using pdb for interactive debugging
- Handling specific exceptions for network requests
- Using post-mortem debugging for unexpected exceptions

Conclusion

Error handling and debugging are essential skills for writing robust and reliable Python code. By mastering try-except blocks, understanding common exceptions, and utilizing various debugging techniques, you'll be better equipped to handle errors gracefully and quickly identify and fix issues in your programs.

Remember that effective error handling is about anticipating potential issues and providing meaningful feedback or recovery mechanisms. Debugging, on the other hand, is a systematic process of identifying the root cause of an issue. Both skills improve with practice and experience.

As you continue your Python journey, make it a habit to incorporate error handling in your code and familiarize yourself with debugging tools. This will not only make your code more robust but also save you time and frustration in the long run.

In the next chapter, we'll explore object-oriented programming in Python, which will introduce you to a powerful paradigm for organizing and structuring your code.

Chapter 9: Object-Oriented Programming Basics

Object-Oriented Programming (OOP) is a programming paradigm that organizes code into objects, which are instances of classes. This chapter will introduce you to the fundamental concepts of OOP in Python, including classes and objects, inheritance and polymorphism, and encapsulation and abstraction.

Classes and Objects

In OOP, a class is a blueprint for creating objects. It defines a set of attributes and methods that the objects of that class will have.

Defining a Class

To define a class in Python, use the class keyword:

```python
Copy
class Dog:
def __init__(self, name, age):
self.name = name
self.age = age

    def bark(self):
```

```
print(f"{self.name}
  says: Woof!")
```

In this example:

- Dog is the class name.
- __init__ is a special method (constructor) that initializes the object.
- self refers to the instance of the class.
- name and age are attributes of the class.
- bark is a method of the class.

Creating Objects

An object is an instance of a class. To create an object, you call the class as if it were a function:

```python
Copy
my_dog = Dog("Buddy", 3)
```

Accessing Attributes and Methods

You can access attributes and methods of an object using dot notation:

```python
Copy
print(my_dog.name)
 # Output: Buddy
my_dog.bark()
   # Output: Buddy says: Woof!
```

Class Variables vs. Instance Variables

Class variables are shared by all instances of a class, while instance variables are unique to each instance:

```python
Copy
class Cat:
species = "Felis catus"
  # Class variable

def __init__(self, name):
self.name = name
# Instance variable

cat1 = Cat("Whiskers")
cat2 = Cat("Mittens")

print(Cat.species)
  # Output: Felis catus
print(cat1.name)
  # Output: Whiskers
print(cat2.name)
  # Output: Mittens
```

Class Methods and Static Methods

Class methods and static methods are methods that are bound to the class rather than its instances:

```python
Copy
class MathOperations:
    @classmethod
    def add(cls, x, y):
return x + y
```

```
@staticmethod
def multiply(x, y):
return x * y

print(MathOperations.
add(5, 3))
     # Output: 8
print(MathOperations.
multiply(4, 2))
# Output: 8
```

Class methods receive the class as an implicit first argument, while static methods don't receive an implicit first argument.

Inheritance and Polymorphism

Inheritance allows a class to inherit attributes and methods from another class. Polymorphism allows objects of different classes to be treated as objects of a common base class.

Inheritance

To create a class that inherits from another class, specify the parent class in parentheses after the child class name:

```
python
Copy
class Animal:
def __init__(self, name):
self.name = name

def speak(self):
pass

class Dog(Animal):
```

```python
def speak(self):
return f"{self.name} says Woof!"

class Cat(Animal):
def speak(self):
return f"{self.name} says Meow!"

dog = Dog("Buddy")
cat = Cat("Whiskers")

print(dog.speak())
 # Output: Buddy says Woof!
print(cat.speak())
 # Output: Whiskers says Meow!
```

In this example, Dog and Cat are subclasses of Animal, and they override the speak method.

Multiple Inheritance

Python supports multiple inheritance, allowing a class to inherit from multiple parent classes:

```python
python
Copy
class Flyable:
    def fly(self):
print("Flying...")

class Swimmable:
def swim(self):
print("Swimming...")

class Duck(Animal,
 Flyable, Swimmable):
def speak(self):
return f"{self.name}
```

```
says Quack!"

duck = Duck("Donald")
duck.speak()
 # Output: Donald says Quack!
duck.fly()
 # Output: Flying...
duck.swim()
 # Output: Swimming...
```

Polymorphism

Polymorphism allows us to use a single interface to represent different underlying forms (data types or classes). In Python, this is often achieved through method overriding and duck typing.

Method overriding:

```python
Copy
def animal_sound(animal):
    print(animal.speak())

dog = Dog("Buddy")
cat = Cat("Whiskers")

animal_sound(dog)
 # Output: Buddy says Woof!
animal_sound(cat)
# Output: Whiskers says Meow!
```

Duck typing:

```python
Copy
```

```python
class Duck:
    def fly(self):
print("Duck flying")

class Airplane:
def fly(self):
print("Airplane flying")

def lift_off(entity):
entity.fly()

duck = Duck()
airplane = Airplane()

lift_off(duck)
# Output: Duck flying
lift_off(airplane)
# Output: Airplane flying
```

In this example, lift_off doesn't care about the type of entity, only that it has a fly method.

The super() Function

The super() function is used to call methods from a parent class:

```python
python
Copy
class ParentClass:
def greet(self):
print("Hello from ParentClass")

class ChildClass(ParentClass):
    def greet(self):
super().greet()
print("Hello from ChildClass")
```

```
child = ChildClass()
child.greet()
# Output:
# Hello from ParentClass
# Hello from ChildClass
```

Encapsulation and Abstraction

Encapsulation and abstraction are key principles in OOP that help in creating more organized and maintainable code.

Encapsulation

Encapsulation is the bundling of data and the methods that operate on that data within a single unit (class). It restricts direct access to some of an object's components, which is a means of preventing accidental interference and misuse of the methods and data.

In Python, encapsulation is often implemented using private and protected attributes:

```python
Copy
class BankAccount:
    def __init__(self, balance):
self.__balance =
 balance  # Private attribute

def deposit(self, amount):
if amount > 0:
self.__balance += amount

    def withdraw(self, amount):
if 0 < amount <= self.__balance:
self.__balance -= amount
```

```
        else:
    print("Insufficient funds")

    def get_balance(self):
    return self.__balance

    account = BankAccount(1000)
    account.deposit(500)
    account.withdraw(200)
    print(account.get_balance())
     # Output: 1300
```

In this example, __balance is a private attribute that can't be accessed directly from outside the class. Instead, we provide methods to interact with it.

Name Mangling

Python uses name mangling for attributes that start with double underscores. This means that __balance is actually stored as _BankAccount__balance:

```python
Copy
print(account._BankAccount
__balance)
  # Output: 1300
```

While it's possible to access private attributes this way, it's generally considered bad practice and should be avoided.

Property Decorators

Property decorators provide a way to customize access to attributes:

```python
Copy
```

```python
class Person:
    def __init__(self, name):
        self.__name = name

    @property
def name(self):
return self.__name

@name.setter
def name(self, value):
if isinstance(value, str)
 and len(value) > 0:
self.__name = value
else:
print("Invalid name")

person = Person("Alice")
print(person.name)
# Output: Alice
person.name = "Bob"
print(person.name)
 # Output: Bob
person.name = ""
 # Output: Invalid name
```

The @property decorator allows us to access name as if it were a simple attribute, while the @name.setter decorator allows us to add validation when setting the value.

Abstraction

Abstraction is the process of hiding the complex implementation details and showing only the necessary features of an object. In Python, abstraction can be achieved through abstract base classes and interfaces.

```python
Copy
from abc import ABC, abstractmethod

class Shape(ABC):
@abstractmethod
def area(self):
        pass

@abstractmethod
def perimeter(self):
pass

class Rectangle(Shape):
def __init__
(self, width, height):
self.width = width
self.height = height

def area(self):
return self.width * self.height

def perimeter(self):
return 2 *
 (self.width + self.height)

class Circle(Shape):
def __init__(self, radius):
        self.radius = radius

    def area(self):
return 3.14 *
self.radius ** 2

    def perimeter(self):
return 2 * 3.14
* self.radius

# shape = Shape()
 # This would raise an error
```

```
rectangle = Rectangle(5, 3)
circle = Circle(2)

print(rectangle.area())
# Output: 15
print(circle.perimeter())
# Output: 12.56
```

In this example, Shape is an abstract base class that defines the interface for its subclasses. The @abstractmethod decorator indicates that subclasses must implement these methods.

Practical Examples

Let's look at some practical examples that demonstrate the concepts we've covered:

Example 1: Library Management System

This example demonstrates classes, inheritance, and encapsulation in a simple library management system:

```python
Copy
class LibraryItem:
def __init__(self, title, author):
self.title = title
self.author = author
self.__checked_out = False

def check_out(self):
if not self.__checked_out:
self.__checked_out = True
return True
return False
```

```python
def return_item(self):
self.__checked_out = False

@property
def status(self):
return "Checked out"
if self.__c
checked_out else "Available"

class Book(LibraryItem):
    def __init__
(self, title, author, isbn):
super().__init__(title, author)

self.isbn = isbn

class DVD(LibraryItem):
    def __init__(self,
title, director, runtime):
        super().__init__
(title, director)
# Note: director is used as author
self.runtime = runtime

class Library:
def __init__(self):
self.items = []

def add_item(self, item):
self.items.append(item)

def check_out_item(self, title):
for item in self.items:
if item.title == title:
return item.check_out()
return False

def return_item(self, title):
for item in self.items:
if item.title == title:
```

```
item.return_item()
return True
return False

# Usage
library = Library()
book = Book("The Python
Handbook", "John Doe",
 "123456789")
dvd = DVD("Python Tutorial",
 "Jane Smith", 120)

library.add_item(book)
library.add_item(dvd)

print(library.check
_out_item("The Python
Handbook"))  # Output: True
print(book.status)  # Output: Checked out
print(library.check_out_
item("The Python Handbook"))
 # Output: False

print(library.return_
item("The Python Handbook"))
  # Output: True
print(book.status)
# Output: Available
```

This example demonstrates:

- Class inheritance (Book and DVD inheriting from LibraryItem)
- Encapsulation (private __checked_out attribute)
- Property decorators (status property)
- Polymorphism (treating Book and DVD as LibraryItem in the Library class)

Example 2: Shape Hierarchy with Abstract Base Class

This example demonstrates abstraction and polymorphism with a hierarchy of shapes:

```python
Copy
from abc import ABC,
 abstractmethod
import math

class Shape(ABC):

@abstractmethod
def area(self):

pass

@abstractmethod
def perimeter(self):
pass

@abstractmethod
def display(self):
pass

class Circle(Shape):
def __init__(self, radius):
self.radius = radius

    def area(self):
return math.pi * self.radius ** 2

def perimeter(self):
return 2 * math.pi * self.radius

    def display(self):
print(f"Circle with
 radius {self.radius}")
```

```
class Rectangle(Shape):
def __init__(self, width, height):
self.width = width
self.height = height

def area(self):
return self.width * self.height

def perimeter(self):
return 2 * (self.width
 + self.height)

def display(self):
print(f"Rectangle with width
 {self.width} and
height {self.height}")

class Triangle(Shape):
def __init__
(self, a, b, c):
]self.a = a
]self.b = b
]self.c = c

    def area(self):
]# Heron's formula
]s = (self.a + self.b + self.c) / 2
]return math.sqrt(s *
(s - self.a)
* (s - self.b)
* (s - self.c))

    def perimeter(self):
return self.a +
self.b + self.c

    def display(self):
print(f"Triangle with sides
 {self.a}, {self.b},
```

```
and {self.c}")

def print_shape_info(shape):
shape.display()
    print(f"Area:
{shape.area():.2f}")
    print(f"Perimeter:
{shape.perimeter():.2f}")
    print()

# Usage
circle = Circle(5)
rectangle = Rectangle(4, 6)
triangle = Triangle(3, 4, 5)

shapes = [circle,
rectangle, triangle]

for shape in shapes:
print_shape_info(shape)
```

This example demonstrates:

- Abstract base class (Shape)
- Inheritance (concrete shapes inheriting from Shape)
- Polymorphism (treating all shapes uniformly in print_shape_info)
- Encapsulation (each shape manages its own data and calculations)

Conclusion

Object-Oriented Programming is a powerful paradigm that allows you to structure your code in a way that promotes reusability, modularity, and maintainability. By mastering the concepts of classes and objects, inheritance and polymorphism, and encapsulation and abstraction, you'll be able to design more complex and efficient Python programs.

Remember that while OOP provides many benefits, it's not always the best solution for every problem. Python is a multi-paradigm language, and sometimes a procedural or functional approach might be more appropriate. As you gain experience, you'll develop an intuition for when to apply OOP principles.

In the next chapter, we'll explore modules and packages in Python, which will allow you to organize your code into reusable and shareable units.

Chapter 10: Modules and Packages

I n this chapter, we'll explore modules and packages in Python, which are essential for organizing and reusing code. We'll cover how to import and use existing modules, create your own modules, and introduce you to pip and virtual environments for managing Python packages.

Importing and Using Modules

A module in Python is simply a file containing Python definitions and statements. The file name is the module name with the suffix .py added.

Basic Import

To use a module in your Python script, you can import it using the import statement:

```python
Copy
import math

print(math.pi)
 # Output:
3.141592653589793
print(math.sqrt
(16))  # Output: 4.0
```

Importing Specific Functions

You can import specific functions or variables from a module using the from … import … syntax:

```python
Copy
from math import pi, sqrt

print(pi)  # Output:
 3.141592653589793
print(sqrt(16))
# Output: 4.0
```

Importing with Aliases

You can use aliases to rename modules or functions when importing:

```python
Copy
import math as m
from math import sqrt
as square_root

print(m.pi)
 # Output:
3.141592653589793
print(square_root(16))
 # Output: 4.0
```

Importing All Names

You can import all names from a module using *, but this is generally discouraged as it can lead to naming conflicts:

```python
Copy
from math import *

print(pi)  # Output:
 3.141592653589793
print(sqrt(16))
# Output: 4.0
```

The dir() Function

The dir() function returns a list of valid attributes for the object passed as an argument. If no argument is given, it returns the names in the current scope:

```python
Copy
import math

print(dir(math))
# Lists all attributes
 and methods in the math module
```

Creating Your Own Modules

Creating your own modules is straightforward in Python. Any .py file you create can be imported as a module.

Creating a Simple Module

Let's create a simple module called mymath.py:

```python
Copy
# mymath.py

def add(a, b):
return a + b

def subtract(a, b):
return a - b

PI = 3.14159
```

Now you can use this module in another Python script:

```python
Copy
import mymath

print(mymath.add(5, 3))
  # Output: 8
print(mymath.PI)
  # Output: 3.14159
```

The __name__ Variable

When a Python file is run directly, the special variable __name__ is set to '__main__'. When the file is imported as a module, __name__ is set to the module's name. This allows you to write code that runs only when the file is executed directly:

```python
Copy
# mymath.py

def add(a, b):
```

```
return a + b

def subtract(a, b):
return a - b

PI = 3.14159

if __name__ == '__main__':
print("This will only run
if mymath.py is
 executed directly")
print(add(5, 3))
```

Module Search Path

When you import a module, Python looks for it in the following locations:

1. The current directory
2. The list of directories in the PYTHONPATH environment variable
3. The installation-dependent default directory

You can view the search path by importing the sys module and checking sys.path:

```
python
Copy
import sys
print(sys.path)
```

Packages

A package is a way of organizing related modules into a directory hierarchy. It's simply a directory that contains a special file called __init__.py.

Creating a Package

Let's create a simple package structure:

```
Copy
mypackage/
__init__.py
module1.py
module2.py
```

The __init__.py file can be empty, or it can contain initialization code for the package.

In module1.py:

```python
Copy
def function1():
    print("This is function1
from module1")
```

In module2.py:

```python
Copy
def function2():
print("This is function2
from module2")
```

Now you can use the package in your Python script:

```python
Copy
import mypackage.module1
import mypackage.module2

mypackage.module1.
```

```
function1()  # Output:
 This is function1 from module1
mypackage.module2.function2()
 # Output: This is function2
from module2
```

Relative Imports

Within a package, you can use relative imports to refer to modules in the same package:

```python
Copy
# In module2.py
from .module1 import function1

def function2():
print("This is function2
 from module2")
function1()
```

__all__ Variable

You can define which names are exported from a module or package using the __all__ variable:

```python
Copy
# In __init__.py
__all__ = ["module1",
 "module2"]
```

This allows users to do from mypackage import * and only get module1 and module2.

Introduction to pip and Virtual Environments

pip is the package installer for Python, and virtual environments are isolated Python environments that allow you to install packages without affecting your system-wide Python installation.

Using pip

pip comes installed with Python 3.4 and later. Here are some basic pip commands:

- Install a package: pip install package_name
- Uninstall a package: pip uninstall package_name
- List installed packages: pip list
- Show information about a package: pip show package_name
- Upgrade a package: pip install —upgrade package_name

Requirements Files

You can specify a list of packages to install in a requirements.txt file:

```
Copy
# requirements.txt
numpy==1.21.0
pandas>=1.3.0
matplotlib
```

Install all packages listed in the file with:

```
Copy
pip install -r
requirements.txt
```

Virtual Environments

Virtual environments allow you to create isolated Python environments for your projects. This is useful when different projects require different versions of the same package.

Creating a Virtual Environment

To create a virtual environment, use the venv module (included with Python 3.3 and later):

```
Copy
python -m venv myenv
```

This creates a new directory called myenv containing the virtual environment.

Activating a Virtual Environment

On Windows:

```
Copy
myenv\Scripts\activate
```

On macOS and Linux:

```
Copy
source myenv/bin/activate
```

When activated, your shell prompt will change to show the name of the activated environment.

Deactivating a Virtual Environment

To deactivate the virtual environment, simply run:

```
Copy
deactivate
```

Installing Packages in a Virtual Environment

Once a virtual environment is activated, you can use pip to install packages, and they will be installed only in that environment.

Practical Examples

Let's look at some practical examples that demonstrate the concepts we've covered:

Example 1: Creating and Using a Custom Module

First, let's create a custom module for handling geometric calculations.
Create a file named geometry.py:

```python
Copy
# geometry.py

import math

def circle_area(radius):
return math.pi * radius ** 2

def rectangle_area(length, width):
return length * width
```

```python
def triangle_area(base, height):
return 0.5 * base * height

if __name__ == '__main__':
print("Testing geometry
 functions:")
print(f"Circle area (r=5):
{circle_area(5):.2f}")
print(f"Rectangle area
 (l=4, w=6):
{rectangle_area(4, 6)}")
print(f"Triangle area
(b=3, h=4):
{triangle_area(3, 4)}")
```

Now, let's use this module in another script:

```python
python
Copy
# main.py

import geometry

shapes = [
("Circle", 5),
("Rectangle", 4, 6),
("Triangle", 3, 4)
]

for shape in shapes:
if shape[0] == "Circle":
area = geometry.circle_area
(shape[1])
elif shape[0] == "Rectangle":
area = geometry.
rectangle_area(shape
[1], shape[2])
elif shape[0] == "Triangle":
```

```
area = geometry.
triangle_area(shape[1],
shape[2])

print(f"{shape[0]}
  area: {area:.2f}")
```

Running main.py will output:

```
Copy
Circle area: 78.54
Rectangle area: 24.00
Triangle area: 6.00
```

This example demonstrates:

- Creating a custom module (geometry.py)
- Using the if __name__ == '__main__': idiom for module testing
- Importing and using functions from a custom module

Example 2: Creating a Package

Let's create a package for a simple text-based game. First, set up the following directory structure:

```
Copy
textgame/
    __init__.py
player.py
items.py
game.py
```

In __init__.py:

```python
Copy
from .player import Player
from .items import Item
```

In player.py:

```python
Copy
class Player:
def __init__(self, name):
self.name = name
self.health = 100
self.inventory = []

def add_item(self, item):
self.inventory.
append(item)

def use_item(self, item_name):
for item in self.inventory:
if item.name == item_name:
item.use(self)
self.inventory.
remove(item)
return
print(f"You don't
have a {item_name}.")
```

In items.py:

```python
Copy
class Item:
def __init__(self, name,
 description):
self.name = name
```

```python
self.description = description

def use(self, player):
    pass

class HealthPotion(Item):
def __init__(self):
super().__init__
("Health Potion",
 "Restores 20 health points")

def use(self, player):
player.health += 20
if player.health > 100:
player.health = 100
print(f"{player.name}
used a Health Potion.
 Health is now {player.health}.")
```

In game.py:

```python
python
Copy
from .player import Player
from .items import HealthPotion

def start_game():
    player_name = input
("Enter your character's name: ")
player = Player(player_name)
print(f"Welcome,
{player.name}!
 Your adventure begins.")

# Give the player a health potion
player.add_item(HealthPotion())

    while True:
action = input("What would you
```

```
like to do? (use/quit): ")
.lower()
if action == 'use':
item_name = input
("Which item would you like
 to use? ").lower()
player.use_item(item_name)
elif action == 'quit':
print("Thanks for playing!")
break
        else:
print("Invalid action. Try again.")
```

Now, create a main.py file outside the textgame directory to run the game:

```python
Copy
# main.py

from textgame.game
 import start_game

if __name__
== '__main__':
start_game()
```

This example demonstrates:

- Creating a package with multiple modules
- Using relative imports within a package
- Creating an __init__.py file to define what is exported from the package

Example 3: Using pip and Virtual Environments

Let's create a project that uses external libraries and a virtual environment.

1. Create a new directory for your project:

```
Copy
mkdir data_analysis_project
cd data_analysis_project
```

1. Create and activate a virtual environment:

```
Copy
python -m venv env
source env/bin/activate
  # On Windows, use:
env\Scripts\activate
```

1. Create a requirements.txt file:

```
Copy
numpy
pandas
matplotlib
```

1. Install the required packages:

```
Copy
pip install -r requirements.txt
```

1. Create a Python script analyze_data.py:

```python
Copy
import numpy as np
import pandas as pd
import matplotlib.pyplot as plt

# Generate some random data
data = np.random.randn(1000)

# Create a DataFrame
df = pd.DataFrame(data,
columns=['Value'])

# Calculate some statistics
mean = df['Value'].mean()
median = df['Value'].median()
std_dev = df['Value'].std()

print(f"Mean: {mean:.2f}")
print(f"Median: {median:.2f}")
print(f"Standard Deviation:
 {std_dev:.2f}")

# Create a histogram
plt.figure(figsize=(10, 6))
plt.hist(df['Value'], bins=30,
 edgecolor='black')
plt.title('Distribution of Values')
plt.xlabel('Value')
plt.ylabel('Frequency')
plt.savefig('distribution.png')
plt.close()

print("Histogram saved as
'distribution.png'")
```

1. Run the script:

```
Copy
python analyze_data.py
```

This example demonstrates:

- Creating and using a virtual environment
- Installing packages using pip and a requirements file
- Using external libraries (NumPy, Pandas, Matplotlib) in a Python script

Conclusion

Modules and packages are fundamental to organizing and reusing code in Python. By mastering these concepts, you'll be able to create more structured and maintainable Python projects. Additionally, understanding how to use pip and virtual environments will allow you to manage dependencies effectively and create isolated development environments for your projects.

Remember that the Python ecosystem is vast, with thousands of packages available on the Python Package Index (PyPI). As you continue your Python journey, explore the available packages and don't hesitate to use them in your projects. However, always be mindful of your project's requirements and the potential security implications of using third-party packages.

In the next chapter, we'll explore working with APIs and web scraping, which will allow you to interact with web services and extract data from websites.

Chapter 11: Working with APIs and Web Scraping

In this chapter, we'll explore how to interact with web services through APIs and how to extract data from websites using web scraping techniques. We'll cover making HTTP requests, parsing JSON responses, and using BeautifulSoup for basic web scraping.

Making HTTP Requests

To interact with web services and APIs, we need to make HTTP requests. Python's requests library is a powerful and user-friendly tool for this purpose.

Installing Requests

First, install the requests library using pip:

```
Copy
pip install requests
```

Basic GET Request

Here's a simple example of making a GET request:

```python
Copy
import requests

response = requests.get
('https://api.github.
com/users/github')
print(response.status_code)
 # 200 means successful
print(response.text)
 # Print the response content
```

Request with Parameters

You can include query parameters in your request:

```python
Copy
params = {'q': 'python',
 'sort': 'stars'}
response = requests.get
('https://api.github.
com/search/
repositories',
params=params)
print(response.url)
 # Shows the full URL with parameters
```

POST Request

To send data to a server, you can use a POST request:

```python
Copy
```

```
data = {'key': 'value'}
response = requests.
post('https://
httpbin.org/post',
data=data)
print(response.text)
```

Headers

You can include custom headers in your request:

```
python
Copy
headers = {'User-Agent': 'MyApp/1.0'}
response = requests.
get('https://api.github.
com/users/github',
  headers=headers)
```

Authentication

Many APIs require authentication. Here's an example using Basic Auth:

```
python
Copy
from requests.auth import HTTPBasicAuth

response = requests.
get('https://api.
github.com/user',
auth=HTTPBasicAuth
('username', 'password'))
```

Handling Exceptions

It's important to handle potential exceptions when making requests:

```python
Copy
try:
response = requests.get
('https://api.github.
com/users/github')
\response.raise_
for_status()
 # Raises an HTTPError
for bad responses
except requests.exceptions.
HTTPError as http_err:
print(f'HTTP error occurred:
 {http_err}')
except requests.exceptions
.RequestException as err:
print(f'An error
 occurred: {err}')
else:
print('Success!')
```

Parsing JSON Responses

Many APIs return data in JSON format. Python's json module makes it easy to work with JSON data.

Parsing JSON from a Response

```python
Copy
```

```python
import requests
import json

response = requests.
get('https://api.
github.com/users
/github')
data = response.json()
 # Automatically parses JSON

print(data['name'])
print(data['public_repos'])
```

Working with Nested JSON

Often, JSON responses contain nested data structures:

```python
python
Copy
response = requests.get
('https://api.
github.com/users
/github/repos')
repos = response.json()

for repo in repos:
print(f"Repository:
{repo['name']}")
print(f"Description:
{repo['description']}")
print(f"Stars:
{repo['stargazers_count']}")
    print("---")
```

Handling JSON Errors

Sometimes, a response might not contain valid JSON. It's good practice to handle these cases:

```python
Copy
try:
    data = response.json()
except json.JSONDecodeError:
print("Response was
  not valid JSON")
```

Basic Web Scraping with BeautifulSoup

Web scraping is the process of extracting data from websites. BeautifulSoup is a Python library that makes it easy to parse HTML and XML documents.

Installing BeautifulSoup

Install BeautifulSoup and the lxml parser:

```
Copy
pip install beautifulsoup4 lxml
```

Basic Usage

Here's a simple example of using BeautifulSoup to extract data from a webpage:

```python
Copy
import requests
from bs4 import BeautifulSoup

url = 'https://news.
ycombinator.com/'
response =
 requests.get(url)
soup = BeautifulSoup
(response.text, 'lxml')

# Find all story titles
for title in soup.find_all
('a', class_='storylink'):
print(title.text)
```

Finding Elements

BeautifulSoup provides several methods to find elements in the HTML:

```python
Copy
# Find by ID
element = soup.
find(id='myid')

# Find by class
elements = soup.
find_all(class_='myclass')

# Find by tag
paragraphs =
soup.find_all('p')

# Find by attribute
links = soup.
```

```
find_all('a', href=True)
```

Navigating the Tree

You can navigate the HTML tree structure:

```python
Copy
# Get the first paragraph
first_paragraph = soup.p

# Get the parent of an element
parent = first_paragraph.parent

# Get the next sibling
next_sibling =
first_paragraph.next_sibling

# Get all children
children =
list(first_paragraph.children)
```

Extracting Text and Attributes

Extract text and attributes from elements:

```python
Copy
# Get text from an element
text = soup.h1.text

# Get an attribute value
href = soup.a['href']
```

Handling Dynamic Content

Note that BeautifulSoup works with static HTML. For websites that load content dynamically with JavaScript, you might need to use a tool like Selenium.

Practical Examples

Let's look at some practical examples that demonstrate the concepts we've covered:

Example 1: GitHub Repository Information

This example fetches information about a GitHub user's repositories:

```python
Copy
import requests
import json

def get_user_repos(username):
    url = f'https://api
.github.com/users/
{username}/repos'
response = requests.get(url)

if response.status_code == 200:
repos = response.json()

print(f"Repositories for
  {username}:")
=for repo in repos:
print(f"Name: {repo['name']}")
print(f"Description:
{repo['description']}")
print(f"Stars:
```

```
{repo['stargazers_count']}")
print(f"Language:
  {repo['language']}")
print("---")
    else:
print(f"Error:
Unable to fetch repositories.
 Status code:
{response.status_code}")

# Usage
get_user_repos('github')
```

This example demonstrates:

- Making a GET request to the GitHub API
- Parsing the JSON response
- Handling potential errors

Example 2: Weather Forecast

This example fetches a weather forecast using the OpenWeatherMap API:

```
python
Copy
import requests
import json
from datetime import datetime

API_KEY =
'your_api_key_here'
 # Replace with your actual API key

def get_weather_forecast(city):
base_url = 'http://api.
openweathermap.
org/data/2.5/forecast'
```

```
    params = {
'q': city,
'appid': API_KEY,
'units': 'metric'
    }
 response = requests.
get(base_url, params=params)

if response.status_code == 200:
data = response.json()

print(f"5-day weather
forecast for {city}:")
for forecast in data['list']:
date = datetime.
fromtimestamp(forecast['dt'])
temp = forecast['main']['temp']
description =
forecast['weather']
[0]['description']

print(f"Date:
{date.strftime
('%Y-%m-%d %H:%M')}")
print(f"Temperature: {temp}°C")
print(f"Description:
 {description}")
print("---")
    else:
print(f"Error: Unable to
 fetch weather data.
Status code: {response.status_code}")

# Usage
get_weather_forecast('London')
```

This example demonstrates:

- Making a GET request with query parameters
- Parsing a more complex JSON response

- Formatting and displaying the data

Example 3: News Headlines Scraper

This example scrapes news headlines from a website:

```python
Copy
import requests
from bs4 import BeautifulSoup

def get_bbc_headlines():
url = 'https://www.bbc.com/news'
response = requests.get(url)

soup = BeautifulSoup
(response.text, 'lxml')

headlines = soup.find_all
('h3', class_=
'gs-c-promo-heading__title')

print("BBC News Headlines:")
for headline in headlines[:10]:
  # Print the first 10 headlines
print(headline.text.strip())

# Usage
get_bbc_headlines()
```

This example demonstrates:

- Making a GET request to fetch a webpage
- Using BeautifulSoup to parse the HTML
- Finding specific elements by tag and class
- Extracting and printing text from elements

Example 4: Book Information Scraper

This example scrapes book information from a fictional online bookstore:

```python
Copy
import requests
from bs4 import BeautifulSoup

def scrape_books(url):
response = requests.get(url)
soup = BeautifulSoup
(response.text, 'lxml')

books = soup.find_all
('div', class_=
'book-info')

for book in books:
title = book.find
('h2', class_=
'book-title').
text.strip()
author = book.find
('p', class_='book-author')
.text.strip()
price = book.find
('span', class_='book-price')
.text.strip()

print(f"Title: {title}")
print(f"Author: {author}")
print(f"Price: {price}")
print("---")

# Usage
scrape_books('https://
fictional-bookstore.
com/books')
```

This example demonstrates:

- Finding multiple elements with the same class
- Extracting information from nested elements
- Formatting and displaying the scraped data

Best Practices and Considerations

When working with APIs and web scraping, keep the following best practices and considerations in mind:

1. **Respect Rate Limits**: Many APIs have rate limits. Be sure to check the documentation and respect these limits to avoid being blocked.
2. **Use API Keys Safely**: Never hardcode API keys in your scripts. Use environment variables or configuration files to store sensitive information.
3. **Handle Errors Gracefully**: Always include error handling in your code to deal with network issues, API changes, or unexpected responses.
4. **Cache Results**: If you're making frequent requests for the same data, consider caching the results to reduce the load on the API server and improve your application's performance.
5. **Use Appropriate Headers**: Some APIs require specific headers, such as User-Agent. Always check the API documentation for required headers.
6. **Pagination**: Many APIs use pagination for large datasets. Make sure your code can handle paginated responses.
7. **Be Ethical When Scraping**: Always check a website's robots.txt file and terms of service before scraping. Some websites prohibit scraping.
8. **Don't Overload Servers**: When scraping, introduce delays between requests to avoid overwhelming the server.
9. **Use Appropriate Parsers**: For web scraping, use the appropriate parser for the content you're scraping (e.g., 'lxml' for HTML, 'xml' for XML).
10. **Keep Your Code Updated**: APIs can change over time. Regularly update your code to ensure it works with the latest version of the API.

Conclusion

Working with APIs and web scraping are powerful techniques that allow you to interact with web services and extract data from websites. By mastering these skills, you'll be able to automate data collection, integrate different services, and build more complex applications.

Remember that while these techniques are powerful, they should be used responsibly. Always respect the terms of service of the APIs and websites you're interacting with, and be mindful of the load you're putting on their servers.

As you continue your Python journey, explore more advanced topics in API integration and web scraping, such as asynchronous requests, API authentication methods, and handling dynamic web content. These skills will enable you to build even more sophisticated data-driven applications.

In the next chapter, we'll introduce you to data analysis with Python, exploring libraries like NumPy and Pandas that are essential for working with large datasets and performing complex analyses.

Chapter 12: Introduction to Data Analysis with Python

ata analysis is a crucial skill in today's data-driven world. Python, with its rich ecosystem of libraries, has become one of the most popular languages for data analysis. In this chapter, we'll introduce you to data analysis with Python, focusing on NumPy and Pandas for data manipulation and analysis, and Matplotlib for data visualization.

Overview of NumPy and Pandas

NumPy

NumPy (Numerical Python) is the foundation for scientific computing in Python. It provides support for large, multi-dimensional arrays and matrices, along with a collection of mathematical functions to operate on these arrays efficiently.

Key features of NumPy:

- Fast and efficient multidimensional array object (ndarray)
- Functions for performing element-wise computations
- Tools for reading/writing array-based datasets
- Linear algebra operations, Fourier transform, and random number capabilities

Pandas

Pandas is built on top of NumPy and provides high-performance, easy-to-use data structures and data analysis tools. Its primary data structures are Series (1-dimensional) and DataFrame (2-dimensional).

Key features of Pandas:

- DataFrame object for data manipulation with integrated indexing
- Tools for reading and writing data between in-memory data structures and different file formats
- Data alignment and integrated handling of missing data
- Reshaping and pivoting of datasets
- Merging and joining of datasets
- Time series functionality

Basic Data Manipulation and Analysis

Let's start by exploring basic data manipulation and analysis using NumPy and Pandas.

NumPy Basics

First, let's install NumPy:

```
Copy
pip install numpy
```

Now, let's look at some basic NumPy operations:

```python
Copy
import numpy as np
```

```python
# Creating arrays
arr1 = np.array
([1, 2, 3, 4, 5])
arr2 = np.arange(10)
# array of 0 to 9
arr3 = np.zeros((3, 3))
 # 3x3 array of zeros

# Basic operations
print(arr1 + 2)
# Add 2 to each element
print(arr1 * 2)
# Multiply each element by 2
print(np.sum(arr1))
# Sum of all elements
print(np.mean(arr1))
# Mean of all elements

# Reshaping
arr4 = np.arange(12).
reshape(3, 4)
# Reshape to 3x4 array

# Indexing and slicing
print(arr4[1, 2])
# Element at 2nd row, 3rd column
print(arr4[:, 1])
 # Second column

# Broadcasting
arr5 = np.array
([[1, 2, 3],
[4, 5, 6]])
print(arr5 + np.array
([10, 20, 30]))
# Add to each row
```

Pandas Basics

Now let's install Pandas:

```
Copy
pip install pandas
```

Let's explore some basic Pandas operations:

```python
Copy
import pandas as pd

# Creating a DataFrame
data = {
'Name': ['Alice', 'Bob',
'Charlie', 'David'],
'Age': [25,
30, 35, 28],
'City': ['New York',
 'Paris', 'London',
 'Tokyo']
}
df = pd.DataFrame(data)

# Basic information
print(df.head())
# First few rows
print(df.info())
# Summary of DataFrame

# Accessing data
print(df['Name'])
# Accessing a column
print(df.loc[1])
# Accessing a row by label
print(df.iloc[1])
# Accessing a row by integer index
```

```
# Filtering
print(df[df['Age'] > 30])
 # Rows where Age is greater than 30

# Adding a new column
df['Country'] =
['USA', 'France',
'UK', 'Japan']

# Basic statistics
print(df.describe())
# Statistical summary of numerical columns

# Grouping and aggregation
print(df.groupby('Country')
['Age'].mean())
# Mean age by country

# Sorting
print(df.sort_values('Age',
ascending=False))
# Sort by Age in descending order

# Handling missing data
df.loc[4] = ['Eve', None,
 'Berlin', 'Germany']
print(df.fillna('Unknown'))
 # Fill NA/NaN values
```

Data Analysis Example

Let's work through a more comprehensive example that combines NumPy and Pandas for data analysis. We'll use a dataset of sales data.

```python
Copy
import numpy as np
import pandas as pd

# Create sample sales data
np.random.seed(0)
dates = pd.date_range('20230101'
, periods=100)
products =
['A', 'B', 'C', 'D']
sales_data = pd.DataFrame({
'Date': np.random.
choice(dates, 1000),
'Product': np.random.
choice(products, 1000),
'Quantity': np.random.
randint(1, 50, 1000),
'Price': np.random.
uniform(10, 100, 1000).round(2)
})

# Calculate total sales
sales_data['Total'] =
 sales_data['Quantity']
 * sales_data['Price']

# Basic analysis
print(sales_data.head())
print(sales_data.describe())

# Sales by product
product_sales =
sales_data.groupby('Product')
['Total'].sum().
sort_values(ascending=False)
print("Sales by Product:")
print(product_sales)

# Daily sales
```

```python
daily_sales = sales_data.groupby
('Date')['Total'].
sum().sort_index()
print("\nTop 5 Sales Days:")
print(daily_
sales.nlargest(5))

# Product with the highest average price
avg_price =
sales_data.groupby
('Product')['Price'].
mean().sort_values
(ascending=False)
print("\nAverage
Price by Product:")
print(avg_price)

# Correlation between quantity and price
correlation = sales_data
['Quantity'].corr
(sales_data['Price'])
print(f"\nCorrelation between
 Quantity and Price:
{correlation:.2f}")

# Monthly sales trend
monthly_sales = sales_data.
set_index('Date').resample
('M')['Total'].sum()
print("\nMonthly Sales Trend:")
print(monthly_sales)
```

This example demonstrates:

- Creating a sample dataset using NumPy and Pandas
- Basic data exploration and statistical summary
- Grouping and aggregating data
- Time-based analysis
- Correlation analysis

Visualizing Data with Matplotlib

Matplotlib is a plotting library for Python that provides a MATLAB-like interface. It's highly customizable and can produce publication-quality figures in various formats.

Let's install Matplotlib:

```
Copy
pip install matplotlib
```

Now, let's visualize some of the data from our previous example:

```python
Copy
import matplotlib.pyplot as plt

# Bar plot of sales by product
plt.figure(figsize=(10, 5))
product_sales.plot(kind='bar')
plt.title('Total Sales by
 Product')
plt.xlabel('Product')
plt.ylabel('Total Sales')
plt.show()

# Line plot of daily sales
plt.figure(figsize=(12, 6))
daily_sales.plot()
plt.title('Daily Sales Trend')
plt.xlabel('Date')
plt.ylabel('Total Sales')
plt.show()

# Scatter plot of quantity vs price
plt.figure(figsize=(10, 6))
plt.scatter(sales_data['Quantity'],
 sales_data['Price'], alpha=0.5)
```

```
plt.title('Quantity vs Price')
plt.xlabel('Quantity')
plt.ylabel('Price')
plt.show()

# Box plot of prices by product
plt.figure(figsize=(10, 6))
sales_data.boxplot(column=
'Price', by='Product')
plt.title('Price Distribution
by Product')
plt.suptitle('')
# Remove automatic suptitle
plt.show()

# Histogram of quantities
plt.figure(figsize=(10, 6))
plt.hist(sales_data[
'Quantity'], bins=20,
 edgecolor='black')
plt.title('Distribution of
Quantities Sold')
plt.xlabel('Quantity')
plt.ylabel('Frequency')
plt.show()

# Pie chart of sales by product
plt.figure(figsize=(8, 8))
plt.pie(product_sales,
 labels=product_sales.index,
 autopct='%1.1f%%',
 startangle=90)
plt.title('Sales Distribution
 by Product')
plt.axis('equal')
# Equal aspect ratio ensures
that pie is drawn as a circle
plt.show()
```

This example demonstrates various types of plots:

- Bar plot for comparing categorical data
- Line plot for time series data
- Scatter plot for examining relationships between two variables
- Box plot for showing the distribution of data
- Histogram for showing the distribution of a single variable
- Pie chart for showing proportions of a whole

Advanced Data Analysis Techniques

As you become more comfortable with basic data analysis, you can explore more advanced techniques:

1. **Time Series Analysis**: Pandas has powerful capabilities for working with time-based data, including resampling, shifting, and rolling window calculations.
2. **Pivot Tables**: Create spreadsheet-style pivot tables to summarize data.
3. **Merging and Joining Data**: Combine multiple datasets using various join operations.
4. **Handling Missing Data**: Implement more sophisticated strategies for dealing with missing values.
5. **Data Normalization and Scaling**: Prepare data for machine learning algorithms.
6. **Statistical Analysis**: Perform hypothesis tests, regression analysis, and more using libraries like SciPy and StatsModels.

Here's a brief example of some of these techniques:

```python
Copy
import pandas as pd
import numpy as np
from scipy import stats
```

```python
# Time series analysis
monthly_sales = sales_
data.set_index('Date')
['Total'].resample('M').sum()
rolling_avg = monthly_
sales.rolling(window=3)
.mean()

# Pivot table
pivot = pd.pivot_table
(sales_data, values='Total',
 index='Date', columns='Product',
 aggfunc=np.sum)

# Merging data
product_info = pd.DataFrame({
    'Product': products,
    'Category': ['Electronics',
'Clothing', 'Food', 'Books']
})
merged_data =
sales_data.merge
(product_info, on='Product')

# Handling missing data
sales_data['Quantity'].
fillna(sales_data['Quantity']
.mean(), inplace=True)

# Data normalization
from sklearn.preprocessing
import MinMaxScaler
scaler = MinMaxScaler()
sales_data['Normalized_Price'] =
 scaler.fit_transform(sales_data[
['Price']])

# Statistical analysis
t_stat, p_value = stats.ttest_
ind(sales_data
```

```
[sales_data['Product']
 == 'A']['Quantity'],
sales_data[sales_data
['Product'] == 'B']
['Quantity'])
print(f"T-statistic:
 {t_stat}, p-value:
{p_value}")
```

Best Practices for Data Analysis

1. **Data Quality**: Always start by checking the quality of your data. Look for missing values, outliers, and inconsistencies.
2. **Exploratory Data Analysis (EDA)**: Perform EDA to understand the structure and patterns in your data before diving into complex analysis.
3. **Feature Engineering**: Create new features that might be more informative than the raw data.
4. **Documentation**: Document your analysis process, including data sources, assumptions, and methodologies used.
5. **Reproducibility**: Make your analysis reproducible by using version control and documenting your environment.
6. **Visualization**: Use appropriate visualizations to communicate your findings effectively.
7. **Statistical Rigor**: Ensure your conclusions are statistically sound. Be aware of potential biases and limitations in your data and methods.
8. **Performance**: For large datasets, pay attention to the performance of your code. Use efficient data structures and operations.
9. **Domain Knowledge**: Incorporate domain knowledge into your analysis. Pure data analysis without context can lead to misleading conclusions.
10. **Ethical Considerations**: Be aware of ethical implications, especially when working with sensitive or personal data.

Conclusion

Data analysis with Python is a vast field with endless possibilities. This introduction has covered the basics of using NumPy and Pandas for data manipulation and analysis, and Matplotlib for visualization. These tools form the foundation of the Python data science ecosystem.

As you continue your journey in data analysis, you'll discover many more libraries and techniques. Some areas to explore next include:

- Advanced visualization libraries like Seaborn and Plotly
- Machine learning with scikit-learn
- Big data processing with Apache Spark (PySpark)
- Deep learning with TensorFlow or PyTorch

Remember that data analysis is not just about coding and using libraries. It's also about asking the right questions, understanding the context of your data, and communicating your findings effectively.

Practice is key to mastering data analysis. Try to work on real-world datasets, participate in data science competitions on platforms like Kaggle, and contribute to open-source data analysis projects. The more you practice, the more intuitive and powerful your analyses will become.

In the next chapter, we'll explore building graphical user interfaces (GUIs) with Python, which will allow you to create desktop applications with interactive interfaces for your data analysis projects.

Chapter 13: Building Graphical User Interfaces (GUIs)

G raphical User Interfaces (GUIs) allow users to interact with your program through graphical elements like windows, buttons, and input fields, rather than through a command-line interface. In this chapter, we'll explore how to create GUIs in Python using Tkinter, the standard GUI library that comes bundled with Python.

Introduction to Tkinter

Tkinter is Python's standard GUI (Graphical User Interface) package. It provides a fast and easy way to create GUI applications. Tkinter is a thin object-oriented layer on top of Tcl/Tk.

Why Tkinter?

1. **Simplicity**: Tkinter is straightforward to learn and use.
2. **Availability**: It comes pre-installed with Python on most systems.
3. **Cross-platform**: Tkinter applications can run on Windows, macOS, and Linux.
4. **Lightweight**: Tkinter doesn't require much system resources.

Basic Structure of a Tkinter Application

Here's the basic structure of a Tkinter application:

```python
Copy
import tkinter as tk

root = tk.Tk()
# Create the main window

# Add widgets and define behavior here

root.mainloop()
# Start the Tkinter event loop
```

Let's break this down:

1. We import Tkinter, usually aliased as tk.
2. We create a root window using tk.Tk().
3. We add widgets (GUI elements) to the root window.
4. We start the Tkinter event loop with root.mainloop(), which listens for events such as button clicks or key presses.

Creating Windows, Buttons, and Input Fields

Now let's explore how to create various GUI elements with Tkinter.

Creating Windows

The main window is created when we instantiate Tk():

```python
Copy
```

```
import tkinter as tk

root = tk.Tk()
root.title("My First GUI App")
root.geometry("300x200")
 # Set window size

root.mainloop()
```

This creates a window titled "My First GUI App" with a size of 300x200 pixels.

Creating Buttons

Buttons are created using the Button class:

```python
Copy
import tkinter as tk

def button_click():
print("Button clicked!")

root = tk.Tk()
root.title("Button Example")

button = tk.Button(root,
text="Click me!",
command=button_click)
button.pack()

root.mainloop()
```

Here, we create a button with the text "Click me!" and associate it with the button_click function.

Creating Input Fields

Input fields (also known as Entry widgets) are created using the Entry class:

```python
Copy
import tkinter as tk

def submit():
text = entry.get()
print(f"You entered:
{text}")

root = tk.Tk()
root.title("Entry Example")

entry = tk.Entry(root)
entry.pack()

submit_button =
tk.Button(root, text=
"Submit", command=submit)
submit_button.pack()

root.mainloop()
```

This creates an input field and a submit button. When the button is clicked, it prints the text entered in the input field.

Labels

Labels are used to display text or images:

```python
Copy
import tkinter as tk
```

```
root = tk.Tk()
root.title("Label Example")

label = tk.Label(root,
text="Hello, Tkinter!")
label.pack()

root.mainloop()
```

Organizing Widgets with Geometry Managers

Tkinter uses geometry managers to organize widgets in a window. The three main geometry managers are:

1. **pack()**: Organizes widgets in blocks before placing them in the parent widget.
2. **grid()**: Organizes widgets in a table-like structure of rows and columns.
3. **place()**: Organizes widgets by placing them in a specific position in the parent widget.

Here's an example using the grid manager:

```
python
Copy
import tkinter as tk

root = tk.Tk()
root.title("Grid Example")

tk.Label(root, text="Username:")
.grid(row=0, column=0)
tk.Entry(root).grid
(row=0, column=1)

tk.Label(root, text=
```

```
"Password:")
.grid(row=1, column=0)
tk.Entry(root, show="*")
.grid(row=1, column=1)

tk.Button(root, text="Login").
grid(row=2, column=0,
columnspan=2)

root.mainloop()
```

This creates a simple login form using the grid layout.

Handling Events

Event handling is a crucial part of GUI programming. It allows your application to respond to user actions like button clicks, key presses, or mouse movements.

Button Click Events

We've already seen a simple example of handling a button click event. Here's a more detailed example:

```python
python
Copy
import tkinter as tk

class CounterApp:
def __init__(self, master):
self.master = master
self.master.title
("Counter App")

self.count = 0
```

```python
self.label = tk.Label
(self.master,
 text="Count: 0")
self.label.pack()

self.increment_button =
 tk.Button(self.master,
text="Increment",
command=self.increment)
self.increment_button.pack()

self.decrement_button
= tk.Button(self.master,
 text="Decrement",
 command=self.decrement)
self.decrement_button.pack()

def increment(self):
self.count += 1
self.update_label()

def decrement(self):
self.count -= 1
self.update_label()

def update_label(self):
self.label.config
(text=f"Count: {self.count}")

root = tk.Tk()
app = CounterApp(root)
root.mainloop()
```

This creates a simple counter application with increment and decrement buttons.

Key Press Events

You can bind key press events to widgets or to the entire window:

```python
Copy
import tkinter as tk

def handle_keypress(event):
    print(f"Key pressed:
{event.char}")

root = tk.Tk()
root.title("Key Press Example")

root.bind("<Key>", handle_keypress)

root.mainloop()
```

This will print the character of any key pressed while the window is in focus.

Mouse Events

You can also handle mouse events like clicks and movement:

```python
Copy
import tkinter as tk

def handle_click(event):
    print(f"Clicked at:
({event.x}, {event.y})")

def handle_motion(event):
print(f"Mouse moved to:
({event.x}, {event.y})")

root = tk.Tk()
```

```
root.title("Mouse
 Event Example")

canvas = tk.Canvas(root,
width=300, height=200)
canvas.pack()

canvas.bind("<Button-1>",
 handle_click)  # Left mouse button click
canvas.bind("<Motion>",
 handle_motion)
# Mouse movement

root.mainloop()
```

This creates a canvas that prints the coordinates of mouse clicks and movements.

More Advanced Tkinter Widgets

Tkinter provides many more widgets for creating complex GUIs. Here are a few:

Checkbuttons

Checkbuttons are used for options that can be turned on or off:

```python
Copy
import tkinter as tk

root = tk.Tk()
root.title("Checkbutton
 Example")

var1 = tk.IntVar()
```

```python
var2 = tk.IntVar()

cb1 = tk.Checkbutton(root,
 text="Option 1",
 variable=var1)
cb1.pack()

cb2 = tk.Checkbutton(root,
 text="Option 2",
variable=var2)
cb2.pack()

root.mainloop()
```

Radio Buttons

Radio buttons are used for selecting one option from a group:

```python
python
Copy
import tkinter as tk

root = tk.Tk()
root.title("Radio Button Example")

var = tk.StringVar()
var.set("option1")
 # Set default value

rb1 = tk.Radiobutton(root,
 text="Option 1",
 variable=var,
value="option1")
rb1.pack()

rb2 = tk.Radiobutton(root,
text="Option 2",
```

```
variable=var, value="option2")
rb2.pack()

root.mainloop()
```

Listbox

A listbox displays a list of items:

```python
Copy
import tkinter as tk

root = tk.Tk()
root.title("Listbox Example")

listbox = tk.Listbox(root)
listbox.pack()

items = ["Apple",
"Banana", "Cherry", "Date"]
for item in items:
listbox.insert(tk.END, item)

root.mainloop()
```

Menu

You can create drop-down menus:

```python
Copy
import tkinter as tk
```

```python
def do_something():
    print("Doing something...")

root = tk.Tk()
root.title("Menu Example")

menubar = tk.Menu(root)
root.config(menu=menubar)

file_menu = tk.Menu
(menubar, tearoff=0)
menubar.add_cascade
(label="File", menu=file_menu)
file_menu.add_command
(label="New", command=do_something)
file_menu.add_command
(label="Open",
 command=do_something)
file_menu.add_separator()
file_menu.add_command
(label="Exit", command=root.quit)

root.mainloop()
```

Practical Example: Simple To-Do List Application

Let's put everything together and create a simple to-do list application:

```python
python
Copy
import tkinter as tk
from tkinter import messagebox

class TodoApp:
def __init__(self, master):
self.master = master
self.master.title("To-Do List")
```

```python
self.tasks = []

self.task_entry =
 tk.Entry(self.master,
 width=40)
self.task_entry.
pack(pady=10)

self.add_button = tk.Button
(self.master, text="Add Task",
 command=self.add_task)
self.add_button.pack()

self.task_listbox =
tk.Listbox(self.master,
 width=50)
self.task_listbox.pack(pady=10)

self.complete_button =
 tk.Button(self.master,
 text="Complete Task",
 command=self.complete_task)
self.complete_button.pack()

    def add_task(self):
task = self.task_entry.get()
if task:
self.tasks.append(task)
self.task_listbox.insert(tk.END, task)
self.task_entry.delete(0, tk.END)
else:
messagebox.showwarning
("Warning",
"Please enter a task.")

def complete_task(self):
        try:
index = self.task_listbox.
curselection()[0]
```

```
self.task_listbox.
delete(index)
self.tasks.pop(index)
except IndexError:
messagebox.showwarning
("Warning", "Please select
 a task to complete.")

root = tk.Tk()
app = TodoApp(root)
root.mainloop()
```

This application allows users to add tasks to a list and mark them as complete. It demonstrates the use of various widgets (Entry, Button, Listbox) and event handling.

Best Practices for GUI Development

1. **Keep it Simple**: Don't overcrowd your GUI. A clean, simple interface is often more user-friendly.
2. **Consistency**: Maintain consistency in your design, including colors, fonts, and layout.
3. **Responsiveness**: Ensure your GUI remains responsive, especially during long-running operations. Use threading if necessary.
4. **Error Handling**: Implement proper error handling and provide clear feedback to the user.
5. **Keyboard Shortcuts**: Implement keyboard shortcuts for common actions to improve usability.
6. **Testing**: Thoroughly test your GUI on different platforms and with different screen sizes.
7. **Documentation**: Provide clear documentation or help sections for your users.
8. **Accessibility**: Consider making your GUI accessible to users with disabilities.

Conclusion

Tkinter provides a simple yet powerful way to create GUIs in Python. While it may not be as feature-rich as some third-party GUI libraries, it's an excellent choice for creating straightforward applications quickly.

As you become more comfortable with Tkinter, you might want to explore more advanced topics such as:

- Creating custom dialogs
- Working with images and canvas drawings
- Implementing drag-and-drop functionality
- Creating scrollable frames for large amounts of content
- Styling your application with themes

Remember that GUI design is as much an art as it is a science. It often takes iteration and user feedback to create an interface that is both functional and user-friendly.

In the next chapter, we'll introduce you to web development with Python, exploring how to create web applications using frameworks like Flask.

Chapter 14: Introduction to Web Development with Python

Web development is a crucial skill in today's digital world. Python, with its simplicity and powerful web frameworks, has become a popular choice for building web applications. In this chapter, we'll explore web development with Python, focusing on the Flask framework. We'll cover the basics of Flask, build a simple web application, and discuss how to deploy your web app.

Overview of Web Frameworks (Flask)

Web frameworks provide a structure and tools for building web applications. They handle many common web development tasks, allowing developers to focus on application logic rather than low-level details.

What is Flask?

Flask is a lightweight WSGI web application framework. It's designed to make getting started quick and easy, with the ability to scale up to complex applications.

Key features of Flask:

1. **Lightweight**: Flask is a microframework with no database abstraction layer, form validation, or any other components where pre-existing

third-party libraries provide common functions.

2. **Flexible**: Flask doesn't enforce any dependencies or project layout, giving developers the freedom to choose the tools and libraries they prefer.

3. **Easy to Learn**: With its simple and intuitive API, Flask has a gentle learning curve.

4. **Extensible**: Flask can be extended with numerous extensions available for adding functionality.

5. **WSGI Compliant**: Flask is compatible with the Web Server Gateway Interface (WSGI) specification, ensuring compatibility with various web servers.

Flask vs. Other Frameworks

While Flask is excellent for many projects, it's worth knowing about other popular Python web frameworks:

- **Django**: A high-level framework with a lot of built-in features. It's excellent for large, complex projects but has a steeper learning curve.
- **FastAPI**: A modern, fast (high-performance) framework for building APIs with Python 3.6+ based on standard Python type hints.
- **Pyramid**: A flexible framework that can be used for both small and large projects.

Flask is often chosen for its simplicity and flexibility, making it an excellent choice for learning web development and building small to medium-sized applications.

Building a Simple Web Application

Let's build a simple web application using Flask. We'll create a basic blog application that allows users to view and create posts.

Setting Up Flask

First, let's install Flask:

```
Copy
pip install flask
```

Now, let's create a basic Flask application:

```python
Copy
from flask import Flask,
  render_template, request,
  redirect, url_for

app = Flask(__name__)

# In-memory storage
  for our blog posts
posts = []

@app.route('/')
def index():
    return render_template
('index.html', posts=posts)

@app.route('/post/<int:post_id>')
def post(post_id):
if post_id < len(posts):
return render_template
('post.html', post=posts
[post_id])
return "Post not found", 404

@app.route('/create',
  methods=['GET', 'POST'])
def create():
if request.method == 'POST':
```

```
title = request.form['title']
content = request.form['content']
posts.append({'title': title,
 'content': content})
return redirect(url_for
('index'))
return render_
template('create.html')

if __name__ ==
'__main__':
    app.run(debug=True)
```

Let's break this down:

1. We import necessary modules from Flask.
2. We create a Flask application instance.
3. We define routes using the @app.route decorator. Each route is associated with a function that handles requests to that URL.
4. We use render_template to render HTML templates.
5. We use request.form to access form data in POST requests.
6. We use redirect and url_for for redirecting users after form submission.

Creating HTML Templates

Flask uses the Jinja2 templating engine. Let's create our HTML templates.

Create a folder named templates in your project directory, and add the following files:

index.html:

```html
Copy
<!DOCTYPE html>
<html>
<head>
```

```
<title>My Blog</title>
</head>
<body>
 <h1>Welcome to My Blog</h1>
<a href="{{ url_for('create')
 }}">Create New Post</a>
{% for post in posts %}
<h2><a href="
{{ url_for('post', post_i
d=loop.index0) }}">
{{ post.title }}</a></h2>
    {% endfor %}
</body>
</html>
```

post.html:

```html
Copy
<!DOCTYPE html>
<html>
<head>
<title>{{ post.title }
}</title>
</head>
<body>
<h1>{{ post.title }}</h1>
<p>{{ post.content }}</p>
<a href="{{ url_for('index')
}}">Back to Home</a>
</body>
</html>
```

create.html:

```html
Copy
```

```html
<!DOCTYPE html>
<html>
<head>
    <title>Create New Post</title>
</head>
<body>
    <h1>Create New Post</h1>
<form method="POST">
<label for="title">
Title:</label><br>
<input type="text"
id="title" name="title"
  required><br>
<label for="content">
Content:</label><br>
<textarea id="content
" name="content"
required></textarea><br>
<input type="submit"
 value="Create Post">
    </form>
<a href="{{ url_for
('index') }}">Back to Home</a>
</body>
</html>
```

Running the Application

To run the application, save the Python script as app.py and run:

```
Copy
python app.py
```

Your application will be accessible at http://localhost:5000.

Adding More Features

Let's add a few more features to our blog application:

1. **Persistent Storage**: Instead of storing posts in memory, let's use a SQLite database.
2. **Styling**: Add some basic CSS to make our blog look better.

First, install SQLAlchemy, a powerful SQL toolkit and Object-Relational Mapping (ORM) library:

```
Copy
pip install flask-sqlalchemy
```

Now, let's update our app.py:

```python
Copy
from flask import Flask,
 render_template, request,
 redirect, url_for
from flask_sqlalchemy import SQLAlchemy
from datetime import datetime

app = Flask(__name__)
app.config['SQLALCHEMY_
DATABASE_URI'] = '
sqlite:///blog.db'
db = SQLAlchemy(app)

class Post(db.Model):
    id = db.Column(db.
Integer, primary_key=True)
    title = db.Column(
db.String(100), nullable=False)
    content = db.Column
```

```
(db.Text, nullable=False)
    created_at = db.Column
(db.DateTime, nullable=False,
 default=datetime.utcnow)

@app.route('/')
def index():
    posts = Post.query.order_
by(Post.created_at.desc()).all()
    return render_template
('index.html', posts=posts)

@app.route('/post/<int:post_id>')
def post(post_id):
    post = Post.query.
get_or_404(post_id)
return render_template
('post.html', post=post)

@app.route('/create',
 methods=['GET', 'POST'])
def create():
    if request.method == 'POST':
title = request.form['title']
content = request.form['content']
post = Post(title=title,
content=content)
db.session.add(post)
db.session.commit()
return redirect(url
_for('index'))
    return render_
template('create.html')

if __name__ == '__main__':
with app.app_context():
db.create_all()
    app.run(debug=True)
```

Now, let's add some basic styling. Create a static folder in your project directory and add a style.css file:

```css
css
Copy
body {
font-family: Arial, sans-serif;
line-height: 1.6;
margin: 0;
padding: 20px;
background-color: #f4f4f4;
}

.container {
width: 80%;
margin: auto;
overflow: hidden;
}

h1, h2 {
color: #333;
}

a {
color: #1E90FF;
text-decoration: none;
}

a:hover {
color: #0000CD;
}

.post {
background: #fff;
padding: 15px;
margin-bottom: 20px;
border-radius: 5px;
}

form {
background: #fff;
```

```css
padding: 20px;
border-radius: 5px;
}


input[type="text"], textarea {
width: 100%;
padding: 8px;
margin-bottom: 10px;
}


input[type="submit"] {
background: #1E90FF;
color: #fff;
padding: 10px 15px;
border: none;
cursor: pointer;
}


input[type="submit"]:hover {
background: #0000CD;
}
```

Update your HTML templates to include this CSS file and use the new styles. For example, update index.html:

```html
Copy
<!DOCTYPE html>
<html>
<head>
<title>My Blog</title>
<link rel="stylesheet"
type="text/css" href="
{{ url_for('static',
 filename='style.css') }}">
</head>
<body>
    <div class="container">
<h1>Welcome to My Blog</h1>
```

```
<a href="{{ url_for('create')
}}">Create New Post</a>
{% for post in posts %}
<div class="post">
<h2><a href="{{ url_for
('post', post_id=post.id)
 }}">{{ post.title
}}</a></h2>
<small>Posted on
{{ post.created_at.
strftime('%Y-%m-%d')
 }}</small>
</div>
{% endfor %}
    </div>
</body>
</html>
```

Make similar updates to post.html and create.html.

Deploying Your Web App

Once you've developed your web application, the next step is to deploy it so others can access it on the internet. There are many ways to deploy a Flask application, but we'll focus on one of the simplest methods: using Heroku.

Preparing Your Application for Deployment

1. **Create a Procfile**: This tells Heroku how to run your application. Create a file named Procfile (no extension) in your project directory with this content:

```
Copy
web: gunicorn app:app
```

1. **Create a requirements.txt file**: This lists all the Python packages your application depends on. You can create this file by running:

```
Copy
pip freeze > requirements.txt
```

1. **Use environment variables**: For security, use environment variables for any sensitive information (like secret keys or database URLs). Update your app.py:

```python
python
Copy
import os

app.config['SQLALCHEMY_
DATABASE_URI'] =
os.environ.get('DATABASE_URL',
 'sqlite:///blog.db')
```

1. **Add Gunicorn to requirements**: Heroku uses Gunicorn as a web server. Add it to your requirements.txt:

```
Copy
gunicorn==20.1.0
```

Deploying to Heroku

1. **Create a Heroku account**: If you don't have one, sign up at heroku.com.
2. **Install the Heroku CLI**: Download and install it from Heroku's Dev Center.
3. **Login to Heroku**: In your terminal, run:

```
Copy
heroku login
```

1. **Create a new Heroku app**:

```
Copy
heroku create your-app-name
```

1. **Set up a database**: Heroku provides a PostgreSQL database:

```
Copy
heroku addons:create
heroku-postgresql:hobby-dev
```

1. **Deploy your application**:

```
Copy
git push heroku main
```

1. **Run database migrations** (if needed):

```
Copy
heroku run python
```

1. Then in the Python shell:

```
python
Copy
from app import db
db.create_all()
exit()
```

1. **Open your application**:

```
Copy
heroku open
```

Your Flask application is now live on the internet!

Best Practices for Web Development

1. **Security**: Always validate and sanitize user inputs. Use HTTPS for production. Keep your dependencies updated.
2. **Performance**: Optimize database queries. Use caching where appropriate. Minimize the size of static assets.
3. **Code Organization**: As your application grows, consider using Flask Blueprints to organize your code.
4. **Testing**: Write unit tests for your application. Flask provides tools to

help with testing.

5. **Documentation**: Document your code and API endpoints. Consider using tools like Swagger for API documentation.

6. **Logging**: Implement proper logging to help with debugging and monitoring.

7. **Error Handling**: Implement proper error handling and display user-friendly error pages.

8. **Responsive Design**: Ensure your web application works well on various devices and screen sizes.

Conclusion

Web development with Python and Flask offers a powerful and flexible way to create web applications. We've covered the basics of Flask, built a simple blog application, and discussed deployment to Heroku. This is just the beginning – Flask can be used to build complex web applications and APIs.

As you continue your web development journey, consider exploring:

- More advanced Flask features like user authentication and file uploads
- RESTful API development with Flask
- Front-end frameworks like React or Vue.js to create more dynamic user interfaces
- Database migrations for managing database schema changes
- Containerization with Docker for easier deployment and development

Remember, web development is a vast field, and there's always more to learn. Practice regularly, build projects, and don't hesitate to explore the extensive Flask documentation and community resources.

Chapter 15: Best Practices and Next Steps

s we conclude our journey through Python programming, it's crucial to discuss best practices that will help you write clean, efficient, and maintainable code. We'll also explore testing strategies to ensure your programs work as intended, and look at advanced topics and resources for further learning. By the end of this chapter, you'll have a roadmap for continuing your Python journey and taking your skills to the next level.

Writing Clean and Efficient Code

Clean and efficient code is not only easier to understand and maintain but also performs better. Here are some key principles to follow:

1. Follow the PEP 8 Style Guide

PEP 8 is the official style guide for Python code. Following it ensures your code is consistent and readable. Key points include:

- Use 4 spaces for indentation
- Limit lines to 79 characters
- Use blank lines to separate functions and classes
- Use lowercase with underscores for function names (snake_case)
- Use CamelCase for class names

You can use tools like pylint or flake8 to check your code against PEP 8 standards.

2. Write Descriptive Names

Choose clear and descriptive names for variables, functions, and classes:

```python
Copy
# Bad
def f(x, y):
return x + y

# Good
def add_numbers
(first_number, second_number):
return first_number
+ second_number
```

3. Use Comments and Docstrings

Write comments to explain complex parts of your code, and use docstrings to document functions and classes:

```python
Copy
def calculate_area(length, width):
    """
Calculate the area of a rectangle.

    Args:
length (float):
The length of the rectangle.
    width (float):
The width of the rectangle.

Returns:
```

```
float: The area of the rectangle.
    """
return length * width
```

4. Keep Functions Small and Focused

Each function should do one thing and do it well. If a function is doing too much, consider breaking it into smaller functions.

5. Use List Comprehensions and Generator Expressions

These can make your code more concise and efficient:

```python
Copy
# List comprehension
squares = [x**2
for x in range(10)]

# Generator expression
sum_of_squares =
sum(x**2 for x in range(10))
```

6. Avoid Global Variables

Global variables can make code harder to understand and debug. Use function parameters and return values instead.

7. Use Context Managers

Use context managers (with statements) for resource management:

```python
Copy
with open('file.txt', 'r')
 as file:
    content = file.read()
```

8. Utilize Python's Standard Library

Python's standard library is extensive. Familiarize yourself with it to avoid reinventing the wheel.

9. Follow the DRY Principle

DRY stands for "Don't Repeat Yourself". If you find yourself writing similar code in multiple places, it's time to refactor.

10. Use Type Hints

Type hints improve code readability and can catch type-related errors early:

```python
Copy
def greet(name: str) -> str:
    return f"Hello, {name}!"
```

Testing Your Python Programs

Testing is crucial for ensuring your code works as expected and for catching bugs early. Here are some testing strategies:

1. Unit Testing

Unit tests focus on testing individual components of your code. Python's unittest module is commonly used for this:

```python
Copy
import unittest

def add(a, b):
    return a + b

class TestAddFunction
(unittest.TestCase):
    def test_add_positive
_numbers(self):
self.assertEqual
(add(2, 3), 5)

def test_add_negative
_numbers(self):
self.assertEqual
(add(-1, -1), -2)

if __name__ ==
'__main__':
    unittest.main()
```

2. Integration Testing

Integration tests check how different parts of your program work together. These tests are typically more complex than unit tests.

3. Functional Testing

Functional tests check if your program meets its requirements from an end-user perspective. Tools like Selenium can be used for automated functional testing of web applications.

4. Test-Driven Development (TDD)

TDD is a development process where you write tests before writing the actual code. The process follows these steps:

1. Write a test
2. Run the test (it should fail)
3. Write the minimum amount of code to make the test pass
4. Run the test again (it should pass)
5. Refactor your code
6. Repeat

5. Continuous Integration (CI)

CI involves automatically building and testing your code every time you push changes to your version control system. Tools like Jenkins, Travis CI, or GitHub Actions can be used for this.

6. Code Coverage

Code coverage tools like coverage.py can help you identify which parts of your code are being exercised by your tests and which are not.

7. Property-Based Testing

Property-based testing generates random inputs to test your functions. The hypothesis library is commonly used for this in Python.

Advanced Topics and Resources for Further Learning

As you continue your Python journey, here are some advanced topics to explore and resources for further learning:

Advanced Topics

1. **Concurrency and Parallelism**: Learn about threading, multiprocessing, and asynchronous programming with asyncio.
2. **Design Patterns**: Familiarize yourself with common design patterns and how to implement them in Python.
3. **Functional Programming**: Explore functional programming concepts in Python, including higher-order functions, closures, and decorators.
4. **Machine Learning and Data Science**: Dive into libraries like NumPy, Pandas, Scikit-learn, and TensorFlow.
5. **Web Development Frameworks**: Explore more advanced features of Flask, or learn other frameworks like Django or FastAPI.
6. **Database Programming**: Learn about ORM (Object-Relational Mapping) with libraries like SQLAlchemy.
7. **Network Programming**: Understand socket programming and network protocols.
8. **GUI Development**: Explore more advanced GUI frameworks like PyQt or Kivy.
9. **Game Development**: Try game development with Pygame or Panda3D.
10. **Cybersecurity**: Learn about using Python for ethical hacking and security testing.

Resources for Further Learning

1. **Books**:

- "Fluent Python" by Luciano Ramalho
- "Python Cookbook" by David Beazley and Brian K. Jones
- "Effective Python" by Brett Slatkin

1. **Online Courses**:

- Coursera's "Python for Everybody" specialization
- edX's "Introduction to Computer Science and Programming Using Python"
- Real Python (realpython.com) tutorials

1. **Websites and Blogs**:

- Official Python documentation (docs.python.org)
- Python Weekly newsletter
- Planet Python (planetpython.org)

1. **Practice Platforms**:

- LeetCode
- HackerRank
- Project Euler

1. **Conferences**:

- PyCon
- EuroPython

1. **Open Source Contributions**:

- Contribute to Python libraries on GitHub
- Participate in Python's development (bugs.python.org)

Suggested Subtitles and Titles for the Book

Based on the chapters we've covered, here are some suggestions for subtitles and titles for the book:

Titles:

1. "Python Mastery: From Beginner to Advanced"
2. "The Complete Python Programming Guide"
3. "Python Unleashed: A Comprehensive Learning Journey"
4. "Python in Practice: Building Real-World Applications"
5. "The Python Programmer's Handbook"

Subtitles:

1. "A Step-by-Step Guide to Becoming a Python Expert"
2. "Mastering Python from Basics to Advanced Concepts"
3. "Practical Python Programming for Real-World Projects"
4. "Comprehensive Python Training for Beginners and Beyond"
5. "Your Ultimate Guide to Python Programming Excellence"

Combined Title and Subtitle Examples:

1. "Python Mastery: From Beginner to Advanced A Step-by-Step Guide to Becoming a Python Expert"
2. "The Complete Python Programming Guide: Mastering Python from Basics to Advanced Concepts"
3. "Python Unleashed: A Comprehensive Learning Journey Practical Python Programming for Real-World Projects"
4. "Python in Practice: Building Real-World Applications Comprehensive

Python Training for Beginners and Beyond"
5. "The Python Programmer's Handbook: Your Ultimate Guide to Python Programming Excellence"

Conclusion

As we conclude this book, remember that learning to program is a journey, not a destination. Python's versatility and the constant evolution of technology mean there's always something new to learn.

The best practices we've discussed—writing clean code, thorough testing, and continuous learning—will serve you well throughout your programming career. They'll help you write code that's not only functional but also maintainable, efficient, and respected by your peers.

Testing your code thoroughly will save you countless hours of debugging and give you confidence in your programs. As you tackle larger projects, consider implementing a comprehensive testing strategy, including unit tests, integration tests, and possibly even test-driven development.

The advanced topics we've touched on are just the tip of the iceberg. Python's ecosystem is vast and growing. Whether you're interested in web development, data science, artificial intelligence, or any other field, there's likely a Python library or framework to support your goals.

Remember to engage with the Python community. Attend local Python meetups or conferences, participate in online forums, and consider contributing to open-source projects. The Python community is known for being welcoming and supportive, and engaging with other programmers can accelerate your learning and open up new opportunities.

Finally, the most important practice is to keep coding. Build projects, solve problems, and challenge yourself. Every line of code you write is an opportunity to learn and improve.

Thank you for joining me on this Python journey. I hope this book has provided you with a solid foundation and the tools to continue growing as a Python programmer. Happy coding, and may your Python adventures be rewarding and enjoyable!